NEW JERSEY
Meadowlands

NEW JERSEY *Meadowlands*

A HISTORY

Robert Ceberio & Ron Kase

THE History PRESS

Published by The History Press
Charleston, SC 29403
www.historypress.net

First published 2015

Manufactured in the United States

ISBN 978.1.62619.733.6

Library of Congress Control Number: 2015937158

To my wife, Carol, and my children—Matthew, Luke, Katherine and Jodi—who inspired me. To my grandchildren, Julian and Destinee. I hope I accomplished something you can be proud of for a long time.

To Clifford Goldman, George Cascio, Gary Rosesweig, Chett Mattson, Rich Roberts, William McDowell and Anthony Scardino Jr.—the visionaries, pioneers and leaders of the Meadowlands.

To the New Jersey Meadowlands Commission staff—a group of brilliant and creative individuals who made the commission an important and effective agency that served the public interest.

In memory of Deborah Coupe Rios, a devoted member of the Meadowlands Environment Center's education team.

CONTENTS

FOREWORD

This book details all of the history, politics and economics that brought the Meadowlands region to the brink of destruction and then how, through the dedication of private and public organizations and individuals, it has emerged as a vital, dynamic and environmentally balanced place. While we should remember our history, it's the time to move ahead, not just by attempting to solve problems but also by renewing our commitment, creating new opportunities, identifying trends and connecting with emerging economic innovations.

Similar to other districts and cities that are working hard to reestablish themselves as attractive places for residential living and centers for commerce, the Meadowlands region's leadership must seriously plan to institute new and innovative transportation systems to better connect the area to New York City and the rest of our state. Without an automobile, there is little mobility for the region's residents. Local transportation systems—including light rail, monorail, bus systems and carefully planned roads and overpasses that reduce traffic congestion—are the keys to make the Meadowlands a great economic engine for years to come. We must begin the process of implementing these solutions to discover what will be best for the region's population.

The Meadowlands Sports and Entertainment Complex is still the epicenter of economic activity and can provide renewed regional investment and employment growth with the successful redevelopment of the entire complex as a nucleus for the area. We all are hopeful that the newly configured Meadowlands Regional Commission will provide leadership in establishing the Meadowlands region as a worldwide brand stemming from major events that take place in the Meadowlands. However, the region's value must be communicated through destination marketing in a uniform manner by public and private entities.

The introduction of the expanded Meadowlands Liberty Region as a primary destination for conventions, conferences and entertainment still has a way to go to become a reality. Effective marketing will raise the profile of the Meadowlands Liberty Region not only as a destination but also as a place worthy of new investment, which will have long-lasting and positive effects on the local economy. Programs to improve the visitor experience can be implemented. Hospitality training should be based on surveys, consumer research and visitor perceptions about their experience in our region. With the national economic picture improving almost daily, the strategic location of the Meadowlands places the region in an ideal position for positive growth. We have only to seize the day.

JIM KIRKOS

Chief executive officer of the Meadowlands Regional Chamber of Commerce, an advocacy group of businesses and voluntary organizations in and around the Meadowlands region

ACKNOWLEDGEMENTS

Throughout the process of writing this book of the history of the Meadowlands region, the authors have had encouragement from several individuals who are intimately connected with the life and times of this unique place in New Jersey. Jim Kirkos, CEO of the Meadowlands Regional Chamber of Commerce, and Wayne Hasenbaig, president of the Meadowlands Regional Commission, have contributed their wit and wisdom to the project. Dr. Francisco Artigas, director of the Meadowlands Environmental Research Institute, and Dr. Ildiko Pechman, senior environmental scientist at the New Jersey Meadowlands Commission, provided us with images from the public files. Lisa Trenshel from the Meadowlands Regional Chamber of Commerce and Helen Strus from the Meadowlands Regional Commission made all of their photo files available to us. The interview with former mayor of Secaucus Paul Amico provided historical insight about the early days of the relationship between his community and the Meadowlands Commission. Mayor Amico probably understands better than almost anyone the changes that have happened in the Meadowlands over many decades. We appreciate the fine article on blue claw crabs written by Dr. Angela Cristini. Thanks also to Joe and Maureen Kopczynski, Chris Schifano and Tom Austin for loaning their photographs. Special thanks go to Whitney Landis, our commissioning editor at The History Press, for her support and great patience, and to Katie Stitely, our production editor, for smoothing out the bumps in our manuscript, which was accomplished with great speed and talented editing.

Introduction

DEFINING THE MEADOWLANDS REGION

If you are driving south on Route 17, the foothills of northern Bergen County give way to a flat plain just below Hasbrouck Heights where the Bendix Diner has stood since 1938. Route 17 was once a sleepy two-lane road called Route 2 that probably followed an Indian trail begun hundreds of years ago. The route wound through a dozen small communities until the late 1980s, when the road was widened to six lanes, elevated in places and cross streets were eliminated or replaced by jug handle turns. Now a highway with lots of commerce on each side, the route continues into the heart of the New Jersey Meadowlands region, where it meets up with Route 3, an east–west highway stretching from the Lincoln Tunnel west to Clifton in Passaic County. Route 3 provides the main access to the Meadowlands Sports Complex, the Lautenberg Rail Station in Secaucus, the New Jersey Turnpike and the great Meadowlands marsh.

In the late 1600s, when the Dutch settlers on the island of Manhattan rowed across the Hudson River searching for land on which to grow hay for their livestock, the marsh was actually a vast forest of Atlantic White Cedar, an evergreen tree variety that quickly multiplies in coastal wetlands. The Dutch cut down the white cedars and grew salt hay in their place. Thus began the practice of neglectful treatment of the marsh, which experienced ecological ruin over the next three centuries until regulation, laws and community activism restored the thirty-square-mile area to a functioning ecosystem. Today, about 260 different species of birds live in the marsh, and it is an important East Coast flyover and preserve for migratory birds.

Snowy egrets in the Kingsland Impoundment, attesting to the present water quality. *Courtesy of the New Jersey Meadowlands Commission.*

Wonderful examples of the species include the American white pelican—yes, pelicans in New Jersey—and about 35 different varieties on the endangered bird list. Happily, marine life has been restored after it was decimated by decades of indiscriminate chemical and ordinary garbage dumping into the marsh's waterways. The varieties of shellfish and finfish have been growing, as evidenced by studies conducted by marine scientists associated with the New Jersey Hackensack Meadowlands Development Commission (called the HMDC or Meadowlands Commission) and colleges and universities in the region.

In 1969, the state legislature passed the Hackensack Meadowlands Reclamation and Development Act establishing the New Jersey Meadowlands Commission. The commission became the land use planning and permitting authority for the fourteen communities that make up the Meadowlands District. The commission enacted its own regulations even before the federal Clean Water Act as it pertained to controlling and preventing waste of any sort from entering the district's waterways. This was the beginning of the protection of the remaining marshland, one of

As seen from the New Jersey Turnpike looking across the clean waters of the Meadowlands, the New Jersey Meadowlands Commission's campus fits comfortably into its environment due to the structure's clean design. The commission had reached its zenith as a highly efficient public agency by 2011. *Courtesy of the New Jersey Meadowlands Commission.*

the most ambitious and successful projects undertaken anywhere in the nation. The commission also established the Meadowlands Environmental Research Institute (MERI), which undertakes studies and publishes findings of interest to scientists, planners, government agencies and the general public. The Meadowlands Environment Center, underwritten by the commission and operated by a state college, is one of the most comprehensive environmental education projects on the national coastline.

Defining the Meadowlands region is an on-going process. The original regional plan identified twenty communities—fifteen in Bergen County and five in Hudson County—that were contained within or border on the wetlands. The New Jersey Meadowlands Commission has worked with fourteen municipalities in its official role of planning, permitting and code enforcement agency for the region. The 2014 Super Bowl, played in an open stadium in northern New Jersey, made the Meadowlands a household term among football fans throughout the nation.

Vince Lombardi receiving the Insignis Medal in 1967, Fordham University's highest honor, from Farther Leo McLaughlin, SJ, Fordham's president and the former president of St. Peter's College in Jersey City. *Courtesy of the Kase Family Collection.*

The New Jersey Turnpike, a major highway also known as Interstate 95, was opened in 1952 and was hailed as a significant engineering feat, especially the sections that were built over the marshy Meadowlands. The turnpike has become a part of American popular culture. Songwriters Simon and Garfunkel used the lyrics "counting cars on the New Jersey Turnpike" in their hit song "America," and other songs have referenced the highway as well.

The turnpike is also well known for the Vince Lombardi Service Center, a place where drivers can purchase fuel and fast food located on the edge of the Meadowlands as the highway knifes through the great marsh. Lombardi, a beloved coach of National Football League (NFL) teams, got his start coaching the St. Cecelia's High School football team in Englewood, New Jersey. He was head coach of the Green Bay Packers and the Washington Redskins NFL teams and never had a losing season. The NFL's Super Bowl trophy is named in his honor.

The district, which covers sections of Bergen and Hudson Counties, is also the home of the New Jersey Sports and Exposition Authority, which was established in 1972 to coordinate the activity of the NFL's Giants and later the Jets in its stadium along Route 3, the original Byrne Arena, the Meadowlands and Monmouth Racetracks. Under the authority's management, unprecedented amounts of income had been earned for the state. A new enterprise—the American Dream indoor theme park, recreation center and retail destination—will rise on the authority's site over the next two years. A new stadium on land owned by the authority and named for the MetLife Company opened in 2010, continuing to be the only venue shared by two NFL teams. The Byrne/Continental/Izod Arena has been one of the nation's most successful concert halls, hosting the pinnacle of the music industry's vocalists and bands in its capacity as a twenty-thousand-seat music hall. Always a venue that offered the most current big names in entertainment, it has rocked its audiences with the music of the Rolling Stones, The Who, Bruce Springsteen, the E Street Band and, most recently, the unpredictable Miley Cyrus.

The Meadowlands region is the most densely populated area of New Jersey, the nation's most densely populated state. It is the home of several thousand small and large businesses that participate in local, national and international commerce. Representing over 1,200 member businesses is the Meadowlands Regional Chamber of Commerce, one of the largest and influential chambers of commerce in New Jersey.

The region has boasted several storied restaurants that have since closed, including the elegant Pegasus Club at the old Meadowlands Racetrack; Jerry's in East Rutherford; Mascio's, which became La Cibelle's; and finally Don Quixote in Lyndhurst. However, Segovia, Angelo's and Mama Angelo's are busy as ever, as is Bazzarelli's, which has been in business forty-six years in Moonachie and rose again from the devastation of Superstorm Sandy through the efforts of family and customers. The venerable II Villaggio, going on thirty-five years at the same location, is a destination for lovers of fine Italian dining. Biggies Clam Bar, known for its large portions, is a recent addition to the restaurant choices. It has

An artist's rendering of the original Pegasus Club restaurant located at the Meadowlands racetrack. The 1978 drawing hints at the elegance of the dining spot that attracted patrons from a wide area. *New Jersey Sports and Exhibition Authority.*

its roots in Hoboken, operating there in 1946, and presently is in a new location on the site of the legendary Clam Broth House, a favorite of Frank Sinatra's. A visit to the Meadowlands region should include a meal at Harold's in Lyndhurst, famous for skyscraper sandwiches and one-foot-high cheese and layer cakes. Redd's in Carlstatdt is where the Palsi family dishes out hearty meals to the political and sports worlds. It was at Redd's that the public announcement of New Jersey's successful bid to host the Super Bowl was made. Redd's location is the site of the first hotel in the Meadowlands, which was called the Halfway House.

Companies of all sorts are found in the Meadowlands region. Wholesale foods are especially well represented, along with electronics, warehousing, personal fitness, chemicals and media groups. There are three large postal processing sites maintained by the U.S. Postal Service in the region. Sizes range from mom-and-pop stores to New York Stock Exchange–listed companies. The proximity to New York City and the New Jersey Turnpike are attractive elements to companies located in the still reasonable commercial spaces available in the region. The district is served by Hackensack University Medical Center, founded in 1888 as a twelve-room hospital and now a university-affiliated medical complex.

In 1966, Leonard Stern—the president of Hartz Mountain Industries, a company that began selling songbirds and bird food in 1926—began the development of Harmon Cove in Secaucus. This great, risky experiment built upscale town house condominiums and high-rise apartment towers, along with a campus for the North American headquarters of the Panasonic Corporation, on land long used for livestock farms as well as a former dump site. The area that had been disparaged for generations became one of the great success stories of American real estate ventures. In fact, the entire region's commercial development stems from Stern's vision.

The story of New Jersey's Meadowlands has been told before in other publications from an ecological perspective but not from the political, social and financial points of view offered in this volume. The authors' familiarity with these areas provides the real tapestry of how and by whom the Meadowlands was developed from wasteland to a protected space. There are many great stories and tales and some surprises. Everything in this volume has been documented either in the press, legislation or court records.

Co-author Robert Ceberio, noted public administrator and citizen "planner," was associated with the New Jersey Meadowlands Commission for twenty-nine years, rising to executive director. Upon announcing his retirement from the commission in 2010, Ceberio was called "irreplaceable" by commission members. Fred Dressel, mayor of Moonachie, said, "Someone might enter your office, but no one will take your place." And that has proved to be correct.

In 2013, co-author Ron Kase retired from Ramapo College of New Jersey, where he served as associate vice-president for grants and sponsored programs. Kase, a sociologist, was previously a faculty member of the New York City College of Technology (CUNY) and taught for several other colleges prior to his twenty-five-year career at Ramapo College. He was one of the designers of the nationally recognized Meadowlands Environment Center project, which welcomes over twenty thousand school children annually.

The Meadowlands is not like other major swamps found on the East Coast, such as the Great Dismal Swamp covering southern Virginia and

Hackensack Hospital, circa 1889, located on Second Street, accommodated thirty-five patients. Note the horse-drawn ambulance in front of the twelve-room structure. Presently, Hackensack University Medical Center, which grew from this hospital, serves the residents of the Meadowlands region. *Courtesy of the Meadowlands Regional Chamber of Commerce.*

The Meadowlands end in Jersey City near where the Passaic and Hackensack Rivers meet. The clean water, bird life and healthy vegetation, which are the results of years of cleanup, abut the heavily industrialized inner city. *Courtesy of the New Jersey Meadowlands Commission.*

parts of North Carolina with its 112,000 acres; the Okefenokee Swamp between Georgia and Florida, which is estimated to have 438,000 acres; or the colossal and most important wetlands in the nation, the Everglades of Florida, which contain over one and a half million acres. The Meadowlands is an urban swamp surrounded not by forests but by fourteen cities and towns along the busy corridor between New York City and Philadelphia. This book is a series of chronicles that provides carefully researched and often behind-the-scenes factual tales of the sometimes-quirky, sometimes-heroic history of a region that's been environmentally abused, poorly developed and then largely over looked, due in part to its odd location. Another title for the book could be *Saving the Meadowlands* because that's what our narrative is about.

CEDAR FORESTS TO INDUSTRIAL WASTELAND

One morning in April 1650 was cold as a result of several proceeding days of heavy rain. A low-lying fog covered the North River, later to be called the Hudson River after Henry Hudson, the Englishman in the employ of the Dutch East India Company who first sailed it in 1609. Hudson was in fact searching for the Northwest Passage, a route to the exotic East, the source of spices and dyes that were coveted in Europe, and a means for merchants to gain riches by trading and transporting the various herbs and powders back to the continent. Instead, he found a fertile land covered with hardwood forests among lakes and streams that emptied into a wide river that began somewhere in the mountains and flowed to the sea.

Five decades later, the Dutch territory New Amsterdam was still a struggling colonial port with a population of about one thousand adults and children. Spices and dyes did not make up its commercial life, as was hoped for by the Dutch rulers; rather, New Amsterdam was a center for the fur trade. The pelts of animals that were almost extinct in Europe were a valuable commodity. They were used for hats and clothing, and other animal parts were used for the manufacture of medications and perfume. Native Americans, primarily those from the Lenape tribe, secured the pelts. Later known as the Delaware Indians, the Lenape established cordial relations with the Dutch settlers who bought beaver and some other animal pelts from the Indians in quantities large enough to fill ships sailing back to Holland.

Livestock brought to New Amsterdam by the Dutch settlers flourished and were depended on for transportation (horses and oxen), food (cattle) and wool for clothing (sheep). The livestock ate a great deal of hay and grass, which wasn't naturally available in the quantity needed. The island on which the colony was housed became, of course, Manhattan and was the origin of New York City. The island's topography was vastly different from today's city. It was hilly, especially after the place where the present-day Seventy-ninth Street extends from river to river. There were hardwood forests, and a sawmill operated at what is presently Seventy-fourth Street near the East River on a fast stream, one of the many that crisscrossed the island. The shoreline was irregular, rocky and dangerous because of the Hudson River's powerful currents.

Peter Stuyvesant, a dictatorial adventurer on behalf of the Dutch West India Company, became governor of New Amsterdam in 1647 and extinguished the first flicker of democracy in the New World begun by the enlightened Peter Minuet, a former colony governor. Stuyvesant understood the need to find a large, flat place to grow salt hay for the colony's livestock not in the immediate area of the New Amsterdam settlement, which was replete with hills and waterways. Stuyvesant dispatched an exploratory party in a flat-bottomed boat that included four oarsmen, two soldiers, a map maker and a planter. They set off from an inlet running to the site of New York City's present city hall. The voyage across the Hudson River's wide mouth to the Dutch-controlled territory to the west took an entire day. At this time, a few trading posts operated in the region, conducting the same kind of fur trade as the rest of the New Netherlanders across the river. After landing at a break in the great fiord now called the Palisades, the party spent the next several days searching for a level plane where grass for animal feed could be harvested.

They found the area later known as the Newark and Hackensack Meadowlands, which was at the time a vast forest of Atlantic white cedar trees that grew thickly along the Atlantic coast. The cedars are evergreens that are too soft for building and not a good fuel source. Thousands of acres of the trees were cleared, and then the Dutch, used to controlling water at home, built a system of dykes to drain the wetlands and planted salt hay to feed and house livestock from the colony. The hay was cultivated in areas known as meadows, which was the origin of the term used by the people living in the Meadowlands to describe their locale. The agriculture continued for about two hundred years from the Dutch time through English rule and into nineteenth-century America until horses and livestock disappeared from increasingly urbanized northern New Jersey.

SCIENTIFIC AMERICAN

A WEEKLY JOURNAL OF PRACTICAL INFORMATION, ART, SCIENCE, MECHANICS, CHEMISTRY, AND MANUFACTURES

Vol. XIX.—No. 5. [NEW SERIES.] | NEW YORK, JULY 29, 1868. | $3 per Annum. [IN ADVANCE.]

DIKING AND DRAINING THE NEW JERSEY MEADOWS.

SETTING A PLATE.

CHISELING

SECTION OF EMBANKMENT.

Diking and Draining Salt Marshes.

The draining of swamp lands is not a new idea. Such lands are not only unproductive of anything which can subserve any important purpose, but they are productive of numerous evils. Teeming with miasma, the home of mischievous and annoying insects they are blotches upon the otherwise fair face of nature. To render them fruitful, and productive of good rather than evil, is a problem for which a solution has been anxiously sought, but heretofore only partially obtained. No system applicable to all cases has been discovered, and only three methods have been adopted in the past to any great extent: viz., the slow process of pumping, ditching, and the erection of dikes or levees. These methods are not only expensive at the outset, but inefficient and costly to maintain. The dikes of Holland are embankments made with heavy timbers and filled in with stone, the surfaces being covered with bundles of flags and

the sand and protected by planking, as well as by earth, turf and stones. In some places wicker work is used to cover and protect slopes, and the willow is cultivated extensively to supply the material for this purpose. In places of great exposure, walls of masonry with piles driven upon the side towards the sea, are used to protect the embankments from the action of the waves.

The fens of Lincolnshire and the Bedford level are examples of the reclaiming of worthless and unproductive swamp lands and transmuting them into fertile and productive fields.

These works are, however, not the results of private enterprise. In order to complete them, it was necessary to seek and obtain governmental aid.

An annual expense of $30,000 each is required to keep the dikes of Helder and West Cappel, at the western extremity of the island of Walcheren, in repair. The annual expenditure in Holland for maintaining its dikes and the regulation of its water level is from two to two and one half millions dollars. Watchmen to patrol the dikes and to give the alarm when danger threatens, and engineers to apply the proper means in cases of emergency, are constantly employed.

As we have said, these measures are only partially successful.

The July 29, 1868 issue of *Scientific American* supported the diking and draining of the New Jersey meadows. The article claimed the meadows were "productive of numerous evils." *Courtesy of the New Jersey Meadowlands Commission.*

Areas of the United States known as marshes or swamps were long considered to be good for only one purpose: to be "improved," which meant turning the wetlands into sites for industrial or residential development. Politicians, engineers and even some naturalists considered the marsh as a place to be "reclaimed" and transformed into dry, buildable, filled-in land. Due to the general public's misunderstanding of the of value wetlands, the great marshes were often used as favored places to dump undesirable items, such as household garbage, rusting vehicles, debris from building demolition, industrial waste, chemicals and paint and petroleum products. A marsh can only absorb a certain level of attack by foreign contaminants before it starts to lose its marine and animal life and plant life cannot be sustained.

By the early 1800s, farming had ceased in the Meadowlands due to the decrease of fresh water flowing to the area from the Hackensack and Passaic Rivers. The uncoordinated hydrology projects—which also proved to be unscientific—drained, dammed and dredged the rivers and streams flowing to the Meadowlands and diverted the water to sustain the residents of Newark and Jersey City, which were rapidly growing metropolises. Salt water from Newark Bay replaced fresh water, and saltwater pools that didn't support the indigenous plant and animal life of the Meadowlands became common. A century of failed reclamation projects left the Meadowlands vulnerable to becoming a gigantic dumpsite. The most egregious dumping was the untold tons of household and commercial garbage produced in New York City and floated across the Hudson River in barges pulled by tug boats and dropped off in the Meadowlands. Prior to dumping the city's garbage in the Meadowlands, New York's practice was to tow the gigantic, heavily laden garbage scows fifty miles from shore and dump the refuse into the Atlantic Ocean. The depositing of New York's waste was heralded as a great positive accomplishment for New Jersey because it turned "New York's rubbish into Jersey soil."

In time, the trash brought to the Meadowlands from New York City and other municipalities was not used for land development projects. It was simply being dumped to get rid of an expensive problem in an inexpensive way. Beginning in the 1930s, using the new roads, trucks could pick up refuse—which included kitchen garbage, furniture, manufacturing and construction debris and industrial waste that may or may not have been dangerous—and easily drive to the Meadowlands under the cover of night, to illegally dump their cargo and avoid paying tipping fees. The Meadowlands was a vast, unwatched area that became filled with garbage. At the same time that legal and illegal garbage dumping was going on, industrial corporations in Newark and other northern New Jersey cities were introducing chemicals and other liquid waste into Newark Bay, which flowed into the rivers that found their way to the Meadowlands, thus adding to the pollution of ground, water and air.

Since the early part of the twentieth century, sewage has also been discharged from cities and towns into the Passaic River. The Passaic is an eighty-mile-long meandering river that runs through about twenty-five different municipalities, including Newark, Paterson, Garfield and Passaic. Up until recently, the Passaic was considered one of the nations most polluted rivers. It brought sewage and industrial waste into the Hackensack River, which flowed into Newark Bay and eventually New York Harbor.

The Meadowlands' fill was also historic in some instances. Known as the Blitz, savage nightly bombing of London's civilian population by German airplanes from 1940 through 1942 regularly caused death and destruction in Central London. The rubble from hundreds of collapsed buildings was brought across the Atlantic Ocean by ships and deposited in the Meadowlands. In 1963, the Beaux-Arts architectural masterpiece Pennsylvania Station in New York City was demolished to make a space for the new Madison Square Garden. Pennsylvania Station was designed in 1910 by the nation's most important architectural firm: McKim, Mead and White. Built of limestone and marble, the station's 150-foot-high vaulted ceiling and its eighty-four iconic Doric columns, each ten stories high, were dumped in the Meadowlands without ceremony.

In 1930, the Regional Plan Association (RPA), the pioneering urban research and project advocating organization, published one of its first planning reports on the potential of the area known as the Hackensack Meadowlands. It's a bit mysterious why the Regional Planning Association chose the Meadowlands for a major study and report within its first few years of existence since the RPA was concerned with planning for the entire New York City and environs, Southern Connecticut and Northern New Jersey megalopolis. However, it did and published a comprehensive study titled *A Model Industrial City Rising on Hackensack Meadowlands*. The report was ambitious to say the least. Its subtitle (*How Swamp Lands May Be Reclaimed and Sites Provided amid Congenial Surroundings for Industry, Business, and Residence for Population of Half Million*) explains the scope of the proposal, which began with the filling of the wetlands with 172 million cubic yards of soil, stone, brick, concrete and other inert material. The result would be a region with over thirty thousand developable acres for residential and industrial

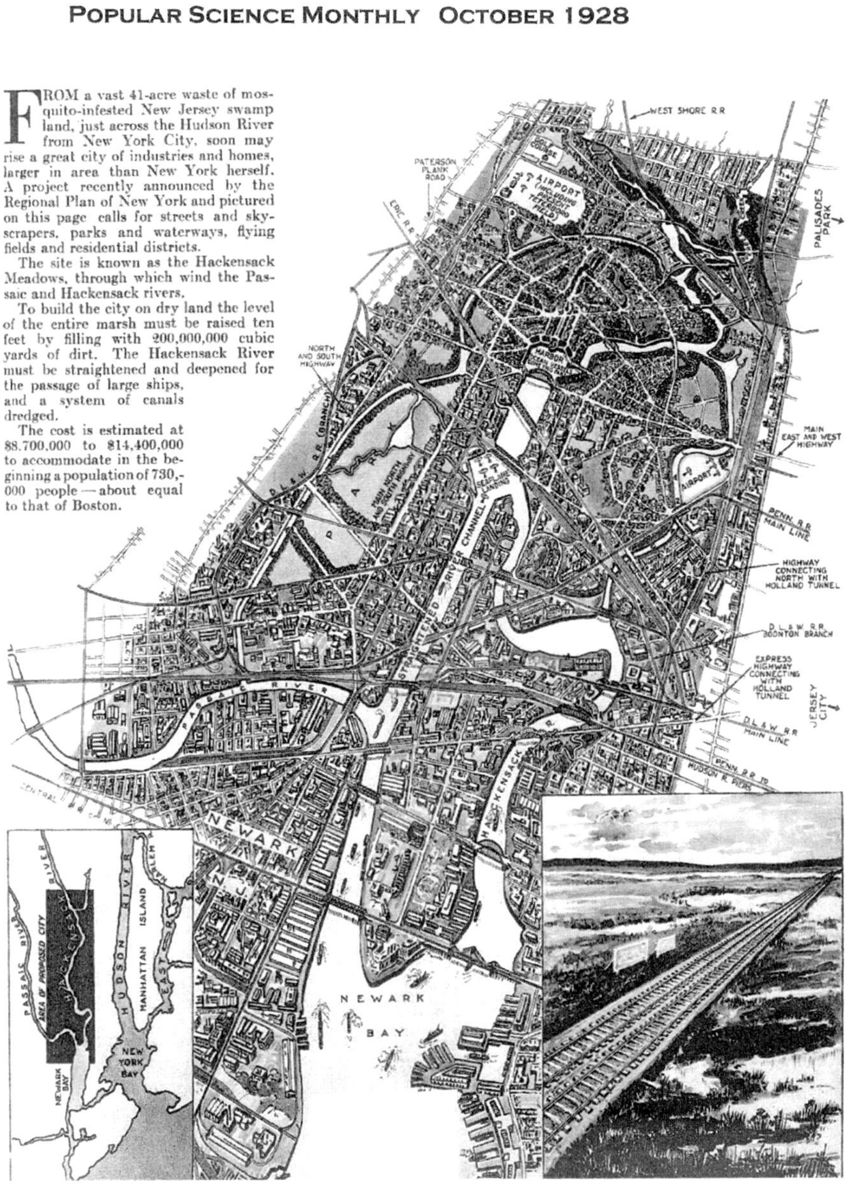

POPULAR SCIENCE MONTHLY OCTOBER 1928

FROM a vast 41-acre waste of mosquito-infested New Jersey swamp land, just across the Hudson River from New York City, soon may rise a great city of industries and homes, larger in area than New York herself. A project recently announced by the Regional Plan of New York and pictured on this page calls for streets and skyscrapers, parks and waterways, flying fields and residential districts.

The site is known as the Hackensack Meadows, through which wind the Passaic and Hackensack rivers.

To build the city on dry land the level of the entire marsh must be raised ten feet by filling with 200,000,000 cubic yards of dirt. The Hackensack River must be straightened and deepened for the passage of large ships, and a system of canals dredged.

The cost is estimated at $8,700,000 to $14,400,000 to accommodate in the beginning a population of 730,000 people — about equal to that of Boston.

The October 1928 issue of *Popular Science Monthly* featured a fanciful article on the "41 acre waste of mosquito-infested New Jersey swamp land just across the Hudson River from New York City." The proposed "Magic City" had many worthwhile ideas, but few were ever accomplished. *Courtesy of the New Jersey Meadowlands Commission.*

use surrounding a great park one and a half times as large as Manhattan's Central Park. The plan called for canal systems, railroad service, bus routes and new highways, as well as an airport to be built in Secaucus similar in size to LaGuardia Airport in New York City. About 500,000 residents would inhabit the new "Meadowlands City," and 200,000 jobs would be created in the region's new industries. There are some small parts of the plan that have been accomplished but not in the coordinated manner that was projected, which, if it had happened, would have been the final act of destruction of the great Meadowlands marsh.

The belief by politicians and the general public that the best use of the Meadowlands was the creation of land for building was nurtured until 1969. In the early 1950s, after the construction of the New Jersey Turnpike, the prevailing wisdom still favored draining the wetlands and covering them with concrete as a foundation for new residential and commercial projects. The Turnpike Authority in the 1960s widened the existing highway and constructed a new western spur right through the wetlands, connecting with Route 3 near the Hackensack River without any consideration of the environmental impact to the region. In fact, Governor Richard Hughes, who was considered to be progressive, predicted that much like the old Regional Planning Association proposal, "the interchange of the Turnpike and Route 3 would become the center of a major new city on the reclaimed wetlands, with housing, industry, commercial centers and recreation facilities rivaling Manhattan." Hughes and most others in public life believed that wetlands were of no value until filled in and built on.

Hughes's opinion of the Meadowlands and his belief that it should be drained, filled and developed was shaped by his experience, prior to his election to the governorship, of occasionally traveling through the wide marsh on a train from Trenton to New York City or on the turnpike in an automobile. Travelers were exposed to thick smoke and noxious smells emanating from garbage dumps along the train and car routes. It was a homely area filled with mosquitoes, and Hughes was embarrassed by this section of his state, which contained one of the nation's most heavily traveled roadways that brought New Englanders south and southerners to New York and Boston. New Jersey had become a national joke, but no one in the Meadowlands region was laughing.

The Early Landholders

The history of the Meadowlands of New Jersey is as complex and diverse as the land and environmental characteristics that make up this urban space surrounded by one of the most densely populated areas in the United States. Just eight miles from Manhattan and bordering Jersey City, Newark, Hackensack and the towns of South Bergen and Hudson Counties, the Meadowlands has a long history and many legends that have survived for generations. Yet so many people believe that the Meadowlands is only MetLife Stadium, the Izod Center or the racetrack. It is much more than that. It is an area of open space the size of twenty Central Parks, bounded by highway and rail access that was looked at as an area of great potential service to New York City. Unfortunately, it was once viewed as a wasteland for one-third of all the waste generated in New Jersey, but it is now a place of rebirth, with the idea that the environmental and economic development can be mutually compatible and not be in direct competition with each other.

The history of the Meadowlands was and is dictated by several factors, including its natural environment and the human intervention that tried mightily to control it to conform to humans' needs and wants. Before settlers came into the Meadowlands, it was made up of a large open area of tidal brackish and freshwater wetlands that extended into Newark and formed the edge of Newark Bay. The Newark Marsh is gone and is today Port Newark and Elizabeth and Newark Liberty Airport. A good part of the Meadowlands marsh was also filled in for agricultural use, industrial buildings and garbage dumps.

Few people are aware of the early history of the Meadowlands, which can be traced to the scientific theory of how the region was formed from the glaciers of the ice age. The real interest lies in the people and institutions that helped form today's Meadowlands. The meadows at one time was a place for hunting, fishing and growing salt hay. The human attraction to this area was also its downfall, as the area succumbed to man's determination to change nature. The abundant natural resources encouraged settlement, which brought change. The development of the Meadowlands forms an interesting mosaic of facts. The farms, pirates lurking in the cedar swamps, ferry crossings, cedar-planked roads and snakes of Laurel Hill in Secaucus are all part of this fascinating history.

Meadows, Marshes and Swamps

The terms *meadows*, *marshes* and *swamps* have all been used to describe the region. Each one of them has a very specific scientific meaning and characteristic. A "meadow" is a tract of grassland used for pasture or a hayfield or tract of grassland in an upland area near a timberline. A "marsh" is an area dominated by low, poorly drained land that is sometimes flooded and often lies at the edge of lakes, surrounded by grasses, sedges, cattails and rushes. Its waters may be either fresh or saline, and it may or may not be underlain by an accumulation of organic remains. A "swamp" is a tract of wet, spongy land, often having a growth of certain types of trees and other vegetation but unfit for cultivation. Looking at the history of the area, each one of them could or can apply depending on the specific point in time.

From where the Passaic and the Hackensack Rivers meet to what is now Kearny, North Arlington and Rutherford and from Lyndhurst to Rutherford/East Rutherford was the Sanford property, acquired in 1668. It contained 5,308 acres of upland and ten thousand acres of marsh and extended seven miles to the north. William Kingsland constructed the first house in the area today known as North Arlington, and he later took over the upper portion of the Sanford property. Unfortunately, we remember William Kingsland by what still bears his name: the closed Bergen County garbage dump the "Kingsland Landfill" and a creek that is now covered by the 1-E Landfill on the Belleville Turnpike that bridges across North Arlington and Kearny. It is not a very fitting remembrance.

In 1710, Arent Schuyler purchased a tract from Kingsland that ran from the Passaic River to the Hackensack River. Schuyler had the good fortune to find large deposits of copper in the rocky ridges of North Arlington overlooking the Hackensack River. In order to pump out mines that would fill with water, Peter Schuyler, son of Arent, paid the English engine-maker Jonathan Hornblower £1,000 to ship him a "fire engine" and a crew of mechanics to set it up. The engine arrived five years later, in 1753. The engine did well enough for five years. Then, it was badly damaged in a fire.

It was said the Schuyler Mines extended all the way under the Passaic River and under a church in what is now Belleville. The legend has George Washington and his army retreating from the British, using the mines to escape from Belleville. The Schuyler Mines came back to life in the 1980s when they reminded some residents of North Arlington about their existence after several mine shafts opened, swallowing backyards and swimming pools,

Kingsland Landfill, shown circa 1968, became the future site of the New Jersey Meadowlands Commission's headquarters and research and education facilities. *Courtesy of the New Jersey Meadowlands Commission.*

because of underground water pressure that had eroded the soil under houses. No one was hurt, and no houses were damaged. But several pools were dropped thirty to forty feet. The federal government came in and provided financial assistance to the borough to fix the problem.

Schuyler undertook a very ambitious project building a road to get his copper ore to the Hackensack River for seagoing barges. He used cedar wood, which was abundant in the area, and created planks to build what is now known as the Belleville Turnpike. The cedar was placed side by side and held up to the salty and muddy soils and the high tides. Regarding the Belleville Turnpike, an act was passed on September 26, 1772, containing the following preamble:

> *Many of the inhabitants of the counties of Essex and Bergen have, by their petition, set forth that a certain highway through a cedar swamp and over the meadows and marshes on New Barbados Neck to Hackensack River is very useful and will be greatly beneficial to the inhabitants of the northern parts of Sussex, Morris and Essex, in passing to and from New York by Paulus Hook; and that Colonel John Schuyler, at his own private expense, hath, at great charge, erected a causeway of cedar logs through the said swamp and meadows upwards of three miles in length, and built proper bridges at upwards of 3,000 pounds expense; and said road will be in danger of being destroyed unless properly covered over with gravel, and*

> *sand that such covering will be attended with the expense of at least ten hundred and fifty pounds, an additional expense too great to be borne by said Colonel Schuyler.*

The Newark–Jersey City Turnpike was constructed in the same manner, and bridges replaced ferries on both the Hackensack and Passaic Rivers. Both the Belleville and the Newark–Jersey City Turnpikes were owned privately and had tolls until the nineteenth century, when they were turned over to the counties. Another plank road through the Meadowlands was built at Kearny Point, adjacent to where the Morris Canal was built, which is now Route 1-9. Other routes were built and are now Moonachie Road, Moonachie Avenue and Bergen Turnpike.

The Vermuele Maps

In 1820, the area between the Passaic and Hackensack Rivers was still covered by cedar forests. Their destruction was well documented. Cornelius Clarkson Vermuele's 1880 topographical maps showed a significant decrease in the cedar area from the previous report (made ten years earlier). By the end of the nineteenth century, Vermuele reported there were 170 acres of cedar swamps in the Mudabock Creek area and 690 acres around Berry's Creek and in Kearny. About 75 percent of all the cedars were gone, and only their stumps remained. There are various reasons for the demise of the cedar forests: some were burned down to eliminate the threats of pirates who were harassing ships in Newark Bay and Staten Island and outlaws who were harassing travelers along the plank roads, salt hay farmers used burning techniques to promote the growth of the hay and landowners burned others trying to reclaim their land. The saltwater incursion into the Hackensack also affected the salt-intolerant trees. The tree stumps can still be seen today on the western spur of the New Jersey Turnpike between Exits 15 and 16 West on the western side of the road. In the early 1980s, a commissioner of the Meadowlands Commission wanted to remove the stumps because it gave a negative appearance of New Jersey on the Turnpike, but it did not happen.

So many have wanted to conquer and reclaim the Meadowlands. The individual or company that could reclaim it successfully would enjoy a

The Vermeule map of the Hackensack Meadows in 1896, from which the present Meadowlands District was identified. *Courtesy of the New Jersey Meadowlands Commission.*

significant return on its investment. Nearby cities and towns, especially New York City, made the Meadowlands a very strategic place. In the early 1800s, the Secaucus marshes were purchased by John, Robert and Samuel

Swartwout of New York City from John Stevens of Hoboken for $200,000. Their dream was to create a profitable market farm that would be able to supply vegetables and dairy to New York City's markets, restaurants and hotels. They obtained a charter for the New Jersey Salt Marsh Company to "drain, ditch, dike, embank, cultivate and improve" the marshes. They reclaimed 1,300 acres. During a three-year-period, they dug 120 miles of drainage ditches and built 7.5 miles of dikes. The dikes were five feet high and sixteen feet at the base. The cost for this project was $150,000. In addition to vegetables, they tried to grow flax and hemp, and eighty to ninety cows grazed on the site.

What they didn't know was that vegetables had a hard time growing in soils with a high salt content, attacking mosquitos would swarm workers, muskrats would burrow through the embankment and high tides would drown their cattle. The Swartwout venture ended in bankruptcy. The Swartwouts kept most of the property even after they were offered significant sums to sell it. After John's death, Robert sold seventy-five acres of Snake Hill to Hudson County for its poorhouse, which ended up having many uses, including as a sanitarium, an insane asylum and a burial ground for the poor, similar to most of the almshouses of the day. Today, the area including the rock outcrop is bounded by the eastern spur of the New Jersey Turnpike. The Snake-Laurel Hill rock outcrop is also the model for the Prudential Insurance Company logo. In the end, the Swartwout grandchildren were able to sell the property to the railroad for an enormous sum.

A more elaborate reclamation attempt was made by engineer Spencer B. Driggs. Driggs purchased four thousand acres at the sum of two to five dollars an acre. His plan was to build a series of canals and dikes that, with the aid of windmills, would pump out water. He also intended to use steam power for the pumps when there was no wind. Unfortunately, muskrats ate through his first dikes. He reinforced the dikes with sheets of iron. Driggs found a capitalist out of Cincinnati, Ohio, by the name of S.N. Pike, who invested $100,000, and together, they formed the Iron Dike Reclamation Company. Driggs effectively cut the tide from the four thousand acres that stretched from where the Hackensack and the Passaic Rivers came together to the area now known as Saw Mill Creek and south of Kingsland Creek.

Pike's prospectus stated that the dikes would last five hundred years, and the reclamation cost would be $130 an acre. The iron plates—six feet long and installed to a depth of three and a half feet below the surface of the marshland—were covered with earth on their upper parts to a depth of eighteen inches. The exposed embankments were faced with stone. The article "Diking and Draining the New Jersey Meadows" was carried in *Scientific American* in its July 1868 issue. Some of the reclaimed land was sold to the Pennsylvania Railroad and others for up to $1,000 an acre. That was a good price. When Pike died, his project died with him. In the end, he successfully embanked 4,000 acres and improved 1,550 acres. Over time, however, the soils caused changes in the reclaimed areas, and the dikes were breached.

In 1897, Vermuele, topographer for the Geological Survey of New Jersey, published the results of his investigations into the possibilities for reclamation of the Newark and Hackensack marshes. He followed this with another report in 1898 detailing certain financial and legislative aspects of his plan. This was the first major public plan proposed for the meadows, and it had many aspects that proved to be exceptional. Vermuele was farsighted enough to realize that agricultural use of the meadows could only be a transitional phase in its development. Some day, he stated, the reclaimed land would serve a more intensive use in the growing metropolis.

Reclaiming the Land

Long known as mosquito-breeding ground, the meadows were, at the close of the nineteenth century, already becoming a place for "offensive manufacturing industries, manure piles [and] other nuisances." Vermuele settled on a diking and pumping plan as the best method of shutting out tidewaters. It was proposed that the dikes along the Hackensack River should be four feet high, six feet wide at the top and eighteen feet wide at the base. Creosoted lumber two inches thick and six feet long was to be imbedded in a trench and would serve as the base. According to these estimates, marshland in Newark Bay and along the Hackensack River could have been reclaimed for $1,265,400. In developing a typical segment of marshland along the Hackensack, Vermuele envisioned a three-stage process consisting of first, diking and filling; second, installation of pumps; and third, industrial and residential development.

Vermuele presented arguments for the creation of a public drainage district to include all the communities of northeastern New Jersey. He foresaw that private interests would be incapable of undertaking a comprehensive plan themselves because they would pick only the best part of the marshland as a matter of economics. Furthermore, private interests could not condemn property, have a tax-exempt status or clean up the area in the Meadowlands vicinity. Nevertheless, Vermuele wanted land to be retained in private ownership as much as possible. His solution was to empower the drainage commission to condemn land needed for embankments and other reclamation work. The commission was to have the power to impose a regional plan, including waterfront development and developing a street grid, but would have a limited power of reclamation and development. Once reclaimed, the commission would be responsible for making sure the owners maintained their properties.

Reports in the early 1900s by the Army Corps of Engineers surveying the Newark and Meadowlands described them as "worthless and a detriment to public health." They compared the region to an open sewer that needed to be reclaimed immediately.

The New Jersey legislature empowered the Meadowlands Reclamation Commission in 1928 to investigate development of all marshes in northeast New Jersey. Its jurisdiction reached from Newark Bay and up the Hackensack River. In 1930, this work was issued in a final report that proposed a land use plan. The plan covered almost 30,000 acres, of which 22,000 acres were to be filled. The Hackensack Meadows totaled 90,000 acres. Of this, just over 1,800 acres were marshes. The remaining were already reclaimed or developed. The fifty-year plan called for 22,000 acres to be filled. It was estimated that the cost to accomplish it would be $91,685,000.00. The 366,741,000 cubic yards of fill to be used would come from dredging various waterways that were part of the plan. The Hackensack River would produce 117,364,000 cubic yards, and Overpeck Creek would provide an additional 15,144,000 cubic yards. Hydraulic fill from these sites would cost $0.25 a cubic yard. The plan divided the district into three sections. Newark Bay was to have port facilities, with some parks and residences, a non-waterfront industrial area and a canal that was proposed for the Bayonne peninsula that would have connected Newark Bay and the Hudson River in a more direct route.

The Kearny part of the meadows was assigned a heavy industrial use. The Hackensack River was to be straightened in order to gain a straight channel from Newark Bay to Laurel Hill. From Laurel Hill northward, the plan called for mixed-use development, including light manufacturing, parks, commercial areas and residences. In regard to transportation, the main features were an airport south of the Secaucus upland and a beltline railroad with highways on the east and west sides of the river and highway spurs to the north of Teterboro and the Over Peck Valley. The east and west elements of the highways were to be connected by a new river crossing at Laurel Hill. Former Secaucus mayor Paul Amico, who is 102 years old, remembers the Curtiss-Wright Corporation buying the property thinking an airport would be developed in Secaucus along with sea plane operations. It never happened.

The fifty-year program for financing the Meadowlands' reclamation and development was estimated to cost between $100 and $200 million with the funds coming from various sources, including the Army Corps of Engineers, state appropriations, reclamation district taxes and direct assessment from the improvement of property and the reclamation commission facilities.

Western Electric's Kearny Works opened in 1926 and eventually employed twenty-four thousand workers assembling telephone equipment for AT&T, its parent company. The giant plant closed in 1986 after the antitrust breakup of the Bell System. *Courtesy of the Meadowlands Regional Chamber of Commerce.*

The Regional Plan Association of New York also had an interest in the Meadowlands. In 1931, in its planning series, the RPA provided maps and drawings showing certain design possibilities for residential development on canals. The Regional Plan Association proposal was an integrated and balanced land use scheme of development. Straightening the river was an important part of the association's plan. The new channel would start at the Passaic River and head north on the Hackensack River to Laurel Hill. It was estimated that sixteen million cubic yards of material could be used to fill adjacent marshlands at the net cost of almost $1.9 million. The plan also advocated the creation of a government authority with specific powers, similar to the Port of New York Authority or a park or sewerage commission. This governmental entity would be free from taxation but would have the power to tax and assess property and have the right of eminent domain. To assist with securing future financing, it was suggested that the state could pledge security to back bonds. Basically, the plan called for all the land north of the main line of the Erie Railroad to be residential and the land south of the line to be parkland or for industrial use.

Canal development was to be the dominant feature of both residential and industrial uses. The other key feature was a 1,289-acre park in Kearny, Lyndhurst and North Arlington. The RPA plan stated, "The best social and economic results will be obtained from a development in which provisions are made for all the purposes of a community, and where industrial, residential and recreational are distributed in well balanced proportions."

Unfortunately, the Great Depression, World War II, filling in marshes with garbage and haphazard development of heavy industrial uses and trucking terminals stopped all the Meadowlands studies, sponsoring civic groups and new Meadowlands plans. The big issue for the local municipalities was never to lose control of the home rule, and regionalists could not come up with a plan that would be acceptable to the local politicians.

Regionalization Versus Home Rule

In the 1960s, state government and the regionalists put pressure on the local municipalities and legislators to establish a structure that would address the reclamation and the development of the Meadowlands. The regionalists feared their opportunity was diminishing, considering the piecemeal approaches and plans that continued to fail. The one collateral issue that was coming to the forefront at this time was the issue of property titles. Throughout New Jersey, the ownership program was debated not only in the Meadowlands but also on any property on which the tide flowed. According to the Department of Environmental Protection handbook on the Public Trust Doctrine:

> *Tidelands, also referred to as riparian lands, are all those lands now or formerly flowed by the tide in a natural waterway, including filled lands. In New Jersey, tidelands are held in trust by the state for the public unless these lands have been conveyed to other uses. Even when the state conveys tidelands to private ownership, they do not convey the public trust interest in the lands. The upper boundary of tidelands is the mean high water line and all lands seaward of this line are subject to the Public Trust Doctrine and are to be administered by the state in the public interest.*

This continued controversy was a major issue in the Meadowlands, especially concerning who owned the properties—those who thought they were owners and were paying taxes, the municipalities, the county or was it the State of New Jersey?

The First Meadowlands Commission

In 1960, thirty-three municipalities were invited to Trenton from four northern counties to discuss the future reclamation and development of the marshlands in those counties. The facilitators of the meeting were the state Departments of Conservation and Economic Development. Soon after that meeting, fifteen municipalities, all from the Meadowlands region, were separated from the rest of the group because of the special issues facing the region, and the small towns feared Newark would control the decision making. Those fifteen municipalities approved a plan that created an organization that would be a catalyst toward regional planning. The Meadowlands Regional Development Commission (MRDC) was created at the initiative of state planners, controlled by them through funding, legal advice and control of the chair. This was the first time under the Redevelopment Agencies Act of New Jersey that an inter-municipal urban renewal agency was created.

The MRDC was the state's effort to move the concept of regional planning from the municipalities to the planners in Trenton. The state was very sensitive to local political issues and how home rule played into the scope of things. The planners knew this was the best they were going to get at that time.

The MRDC moved forward with various studies and historical research on various plans for the region. It also outlined theoretical concepts, such as the inter-municipal sharing of costs and tax benefits of regional development. Additionally, the Army Corps of Engineers was in the midst of preparing a cost-benefit analysis of a flood control plan for the Meadowlands. The corps and the MRDC differed on how the plan should be developed. The MRDC did not look too kindly on the corps' dictating land uses, and the corps became frustrated with the lack of cooperation. The corps ultimately told the state that it would plan the future of the Meadowlands. The state, under the guise of protecting home rule, told the corps that it would prepare the plan on behalf of the towns. The corps accepted the approach, and the state started to implement the plan, with or without the MRDC. The state used the potential of federal control as a fear tactic several times over the next ten years to move the regional planning agenda forward.

The MRDC received funding from the United States Department of Housing and Urban Development (HUD) to conduct various planning studies and reports. The state was in total control of the process, with the local cost share covered by the state. It was the belief of the state that the MRDC was not going to be the instrument to adopt and implement a regional plan. To that end, the state received a second HUD grant that examined a structure of an entity that could grow from the MRDC or even an alternative to the organization. To keep the local interests in check, the state put the MRDC logo on the documents. When it became clear to local members of the MRDC that the state was looking for a balanced development plan that included housing where local interest wanted industrial uses, the split grew wider between the MRDC and the state.

In 1963, the MRDC rebelled against the state and demanded that the election of the chairman be from local board members. It also demanded that the planning process be placed in the hands of local members. The state agreed, which resulted in the end of any further progress on inter-municipal planning.

Governor Hughes took office in 1962 and very quickly backed the need for an army corps flood study of the Meadowlands. He supported the planning process through the MRDC but was also very interested in the Rutgers studies that described a regional planning process and a structure to implement such planning. In 1963, the legislature created the New Jersey Commission to Study Meadowlands Development, and Hughes named his predecessor, Governor Robert Meyner, its chairman. The commission had a twofold purpose: address the riparian title issues and find a mechanism for developing the Meadowlands. It was clear that this was a move to replace the MRDC, which would allow the state a much larger and stronger role in the Meadowlands. The Meyner Commission recommended the following solution to the riparian title issue:

1. Each landowner would have the opportunity to prove, in an administrative hearing, that his or her interests were paramount to those of the School Fund. (Revenue received by the state from the sale or licensing of riparian lands went into a special account for education.)
2. In dealing with a large number of similar easements, an agency could be created to adopt standards of proof that would expedite the disposition of such claims.
3. If a property was considered riparian, the initial loss of local tax revenue would be minimized since lessees could continue to pay taxes on the basis of present use, which, for permanently improved parcels, constitutes the principal source of tax ratable property. Moreover, local tax revenues were expected to increase as reclamation brought new value to the parcel.
4. Existing business would continue without disruption.

On the issue of Meadowlands development, the commission strongly supported the creation of a new state Meadowlands authority. "The Commission believes that the only remaining obstacle to full-scale reclamation, especially in the Hackensack Meadows, is the lack of governmental machinery to formulate and carry through a program. Urgently needed is a unified direction, with the planning, financing and execution of powers, the personnel, and the breadth of vision, to make sense of Meadowlands development." The report further stated municipal control over the development plan of the Meadowlands served a severe limitation on land use planning.

Needless to say, both the MRDC and the state planners were critical of the Meyer findings. The municipalities were critical because of loss of home rule and the state planners because they believed the concepts that the commission brought forth were good but politically unachievable. Because of the political reaction to the report, the legislature asked that the commission go back and recommend a compromise from its previous position. In its new report, the commission stripped the new regional authority of almost all the powers of planning.

2

THE HACKENSACK MEADOWLANDS RECLAMATION AND DEVELOPMENT ACT

Clifford A. Goldman, assistant to Commissioner Paul Ylivasker of the Department of Community Affairs and later the first executive director of the New Jersey Meadowlands Commission appointed by Governor Hughes and Governor Cahill, provided an excellent historical background to the years and days leading the passage of the Meadowlands Act.

On May 8, 1967, Senator Alfred Kiefer of Bergen County introduced the Hackensack Meadowlands Reclamation and Development Act. The bill called for the creation of a new political subdivision of the state that had master planning authority and would be in total control of development in the Meadowlands. The new board of the agency would have eleven members—four cabinet members, three appointed from anywhere in the state without the advice and consent of the senate and four local members appointed by municipalities and county freeholders.

It created a mayors' advisory committee with little or no substantive power or authority. The new agency would have zoning control and would establish codes, including variances with the commission's own plan, and have the ability to pool resources to share in the cost and benefits of development. It would also have the ability to settle title disputes.

Kiefer understood that the introduction of the bill was nothing more than a trial balloon and to start the discussion, even if the chances of the bill being passed were slim at best. Kiefer wanted the bill to be part of his platform for reelection and got good mileage on his trip to Holland to examine the Dutch reclamation techniques. It was understood by all parties that the bill was too controversial and complicated to make any headway before the election. The new commissioner of the Department of Community Affairs, Paul Ylivasker, believed that the bill would have significant educational value. By putting the bill out as a discussion starting point, it was felt the problems in the bill could be identified. Ylivisaker was willing to be the point person and spokesperson for the administration on the bill. He made it clear that the state would control the new planning entity, and the mayors, even with all their attempts at regionalization, could not come up with a solution.

At the same time the bill was introduced, a riparian title court case was heading to the New Jersey Supreme Court. Landowners throughout the state became very concerned about what the court decision might be. Additionally, the Army Corps of Engineers waited anxiously for a land use plan so that it could move forward with a flood control plan for the Meadowlands.

The reaction to the bill was as expected, with the mayors blasting the legislation as not necessary and useless on many points. They felt they were doing well without state assistance and that the MRDC was working fine and should be continued. Additionally, it was the state's fault that Meadowlands development was slowed because of the riparian title issue, which the state refused to address. The mayors pointed out how much development had already occurred without state help, and they felt they did not need help from the army corps for the flooding issues. The state, they insisted, should provide the financial resources to address infrastructure needs. The public discourse on the bill did show Ylivisaker and the state there would be no compromise.

The next attempt to move a bill came from Fairleigh S. Dickinson Jr., chairman of the Becton Dickinson Company, who had been involved with Meadowlands issues for many years. He was a member of the Meadowlands Regional Planning Board in the 1950s and vice-chairman of the Meyner Commission in the 1960s. Dickinson was a very well-respected member of the Bergen delegation to the state senate and very influential with senators across the state. Not known to be involved very much in politics, one of the reasons he ran for office was to address the Meadowlands issue. He was viewed by most members of the upper chamber as an expert in Meadowlands issues, and many deferred to him on the matter. Dickinson's father and Maxwell Becton founded Fairleigh Dickinson University in Rutherford in 1942. The campus occupied the Iviswold Estate, built in the 1880s, which featured the only castle in Bergen County. In 1993, the university sold the Rutherford campus to Felician College.

The 1968 elections proved to be a landslide for the Republican Party; it picked up three-to-one margins in both houses. With a very popular Democrat governor in Hughes and with a strong majority of Republicans in the legislature, the dynamics in how legislation was moved was a real study of compromise and governance. The Republicans wanted a constitutional amendment that would address the riparian title issue once and for all. The vote for such an amendment question would be an easy vote considering they had the required three-fifths vote for the amendment to be put on the ballot regardless of Hughes's opposition. The recent landslides also increased the number of legislators who were pro-Meadowlands. The pro-riparian title legislators were willing to vote on a Meadowlands bill in exchange for the title vote. Hughes was a master at using his office and the press to overcome the majorities he faced in both houses.

While the Republicans and Democrats in the senate worked out the details of how the bills would move, the assembly created an impasse with an amendment to the Meadowlands bill that rendered it useless and weak. Senator Frank Guarini of Hudson County, who was the committee chairman who would hear the bill, was inclined to compromise toward local objections. Hughes's team, headed by Ylivisaker, wanted a bill that could be improved but not compromised. The major issues between Guarini and Dickinson were the composition of the new board, mayors' advisory committee and the tax sharing structure. Ylivisaker and Guarini drafted new language, with Dickinson making the final decision on the changed language. The drafts went back and forth until Hughes stepped in and directed what the best course of action was.

Ylivisaker's strategy was to not debate the home rule aspect versus regional planning. He developed an approach that focused on reasonable people and groups that could grasp the concept of the bigger picture. Ylivisaker took his campaign to every mayor and town that would allow him to speak on the bill. He took suggestions and made modifications but did not waiver from the state-controlled agency. The *New York Times*' description of the discussions with the mayors was portrayed as the state being very reasonable in listening to the mayor's suggestions. It further indicated the mayors were not ignored, and they were indeed part of the process. The mayors found themselves in a position of not being able to articulate the reasons why the bill was bad or why they should continue to be responsible for planning. Only one mayor had the courage to support the legislation, William McDowell of North Arlington. He made it clear that the mayors had the opportunity to develop the Meadowlands in an orderly fashion through the MRDC yet

Youngsters from Lyndhurst riding bikes in the Bergen County Landfill. Note the "mountain" along the photo's top, which is a former dump site. *Courtesy of the New Jersey Meadowlands Commission.*

failed time and time again. McDowell later became executive director of the Hackensack Meadowlands Commission.

At the hearing for the legislation, Dickinson portrayed himself as the steward of the Meadowlands, believing in the principles of local democracy and as a defender of those principles. During the testimony on the bill, Mayor Sarubbi of North Bergen (also the owner of a construction company) stated his company had done a great deal of construction work in the meadows and did not need any interference from the state. He spoke about how municipalities were in a position to give quick approval. The mayor of Little Ferry spoke about how the Bergen County sewer authority took control of fifty acres of his Meadowlands and that his town was left with the burden of having the plant in his town without compensation. When asked by a committee member whether solid waste should be handled on a regional basis, he answered yes, as long it was not in his town.

After the hearing, the committee did make changes to the bill by increasing the commissioner membership from five to nine and the two at-large seats had to consist of one each from Bergen and Hudson Counties. The committee also incorporated boundary changes, reducing the size of the district by two thousand acres, eliminating some towns from the district and making some technical boundary changes that were suggested by several mayors. Ridgefield Park, Wood Ridge, Hasbrouck Heights and Fairview were taken out of the boundaries of the new district.

At the same time, the Army Corps of Engineers, which for years had worked on various plans to control flooding and reclaiming wetlands, became the focal point as to why the bill was necessary. The corps was pressing the state to get the local cooperation it needed on a land use plan so it would not go to Congress to get the appropriation for flood control and reclamation and filling the wetlands. Ylivasaker devised a plan that would move the corps issue to the forefront. The corps was of the opinion that it needed $300 million to take care of the Meadowlands problems. It was clear the state could never cover those costs. Ylivasaker had the Department of Community Affairs publish a document that Dickinson sent to forty thousand

The 1-E Landfill that operated from 1977 to 1987 and was the main dumping site for trash from Essex, Passaic and Hudson Counties. The hill is the actual landfill site, and the marsh was saved from destruction by the Meadowlands legislation. *Courtesy of the New Jersey Meadowlands Commission.*

residents of the Meadowlands towns that "blamed the fragmented and competitive local governments for the resulting hodge-podge of unplanned one story buildings, warehouses and sheds, junk yards and garbage dumps." Ylivasaker addressed the stagnation of "a dead river carrying the equivalent of raw sewerage from half a million people, surrounded by tidal swamps that receive piles of garbage which each year equals the volume of three hundred Washington monuments, where smog and smells and mosquitoes are born." Dickinson produced a film to document the horrific conditions in the meadows and took legislators out by boat so they could experience the conditions firsthand.

Ylivasaker sought and received the endorsement of the Regional Plan Association, the New Jersey Builder Association, various union building trades and the New Jersey Education Association (NJEA), which was interested in keeping the School Fund in place. For all riparian land sales in the state, the New Jersey Constitution required the funds to be place in a dedicated fund for educational purposes. The *Bergen Record*, *Star Ledger* and *New York Times* covered the bill very closely, and reporters knew every aspect of the legislation. The editorial boards of those papers were busy supporting the bill. They liked and trusted Ylivasaker.

Property, Power and Politics

Since 1964, there were several attempts to move a constitutional amendment to clear riparian title problems throughout the state. The state chamber of commerce and Senator William Hiering of Ocean County thought the Meadowlands issue could be a turning point to get the necessary three-fifths of the legislators to vote to put the question on the ballot as a constitutional amendment. The Dickinson bill had a provision in it to address the Meadowlands title questions and had the support of most of the Republican senators from North Jersey counties. Hiering introduced the constitutional amendment resolution the same day that the Dickinson/Guarini Meadowlands bill was introduced. Hiering's constitutional amendment would negate the state's claim to riparian lands. Dickinson did not agree with the concept that the state should just give up ownership of the property, especially when the state would lose millions of dollars that would have gone to the School Fund. It became inherently clear to Dickinson that if the constitutional amendment resolution was not moved and he supported it, the Meadowlands bill would be dead. Ultimately, Dickinson had no choice. He felt that the public could still defeat the riparian issue, so he was willing to take the chance. Governor Hughes opposed the constitutional question and made it clear that it was a giveaway that could cost the state $1 billion for education.

On April 29, 1968, both bills passed the senate with no dissenting votes. The task now at hand was the vote in the assembly, which was going to be a much more difficult road. The Bergen delegation and the opposition leader was Peter J. Russo, of Lyndhurst, who was also a commissioner in the town. Assemblyman Russo strongly supported a proposal brought before the Lyndhurst governing body to lease 440 acres of wetlands to a garbage hauling company. The Hudson County Democrats also opposed the bill in the assembly even though the Hudson senators voted for it. It was suspected that the Hudson delegation was holding its support to get the racetrack in Secaucus it had been trying to get for years. With only two sessions left before the summer recess, the chance for the Meadowlands bill looked grim. With the help of the Atlantic County boss Hap Farley, the speaker of the assembly said he would free the riparian title and Meadowlands legislation for a vote. The newspapers continued to put pressure on the assembly for their inactions. Hughes called the sponsors, local officials and the leadership of the assembly into his office the day before the last session day. The assembly majority leader—Peter Moraites, who was running against Congressman Henry Helstoski of East Rutherford (Helstoski opposed the Meadowlands bill)—offered a plan that would get the bill out of caucus. The bill would be released only if it would be reopened for amendments generated by local Meadowlands interests. With the amendment in place, the bill would be put in position to be voted on after the November election. All parties accepted the plan. Moraites lost the election to Helstoski and swore vengeance against Peter Russo for double crossing him and not helping him with the South Bergen vote. He swore that he would post the bill and make sure that it would pass.

After the election, Assemblyman Harold Hollenbeck proposed amendments that watered down the bill. Hollenbeck's amendments included boundary changes, delay in the tax sharing implementation and veto power for the mayors. The draft amendments proposed cutting five thousand acres from the map and removing large areas of Secaucus and western Bergen County towns from the legislation. The map drawn to show the amendment boundary was an erratic line that made no sense at all. The new tax sharing language was placed in the wrong section of the legislation. With the amendments in place, the bill was released from caucus for a floor vote.

The evening the bill was released, Ylvisaker, the sponsors, Moraites and Hollenbeck were asked to come to Governor Hughes's office. When the governor unrolled the new map, it became evident to everyone in the room the new boundaries made no sense at all and would be an easy attack point. He questioned Moraites's ability to lead and dismissed Hollenbeck as being totally irrelevant. The governor was furious with Guarini, whom he held responsible for the Secaucus amendments, and with the Republican leadership for making a deal with the Hudson County Democrats after he threatened them that he would make no appointments in Hudson County. Hughes demanded that the amendments be withdrawn. Moraites indicated that he did not have the votes for the original version of the bill. He indicated that he lacked South Jersey support. Hughes picked up the phone and called Senator Farley. When he hung up, he told Moraites he must have been mistaken. Guarini thought it best to pass the bill as it was and amend it later. Hughes ended that discussion quickly. Hughes told the group that he was ready to make a presentation to the press that described deals made with landowners. Moraites left the room and attempted to round up the assembly that had just adjourned but to no avail.

Hughes held a press conference and made statements as he ruminated in his office. To increase the pressure, he put a moratorium on all riparian grants in the state and indicated that he would veto the legislation if it were passed. Before the next session, the governor called in leadership from both houses for a briefing with the Army Corps of Engineers. Hughes pressed the issue with the corps regarding the $300 million for flood control and reclamation. The corps agreed to put its position in writing that the legislation as amended would not work. That day, the bill passed in both houses, putting it into position for a veto. Hughes drafted the veto message himself. He stressed in the message that the amendment was the work of special interests. The editorial boards backed the governor's position. When reporters asked Assemblyman Hollenbeck about the amendments, he told the *Star Ledger* that he was misled by the boundary changes. It became a front-page story on the Sunday edition. The legislature accepted the governor's conditions, and the senate voted 36–0. When it got to the assembly, it had only 33 votes. The governor called in the Hudson County delegation and began ripping up papers that were scheduled to be judicial appointments in Hudson County. At the end of the day, the assembly passed the bill with the changes.

Governor Richard Hughes signing the Meadowlands bill. *Courtesy of the New Jersey Meadowlands Commission.*

With the Meadowlands bill passed, the governor focused his attention on the riparian constitutional amendment. He attacked that legislation with a public campaign and legal maneuvers. The campaign went as far as associating organized crime with legislators and a series of conflict-of-interest charges. A legislative investigation was called for to look into the charges. Again, Hughes won, and the proposal for the constitutional amendment was withdrawn. Some legislators claimed that he reneged on the deal to let both the Meadowlands and riparian bills move together. But Hughes was never part of that discussion.

For additional material about the Meadowlands from farms to ruined wasteland over the last three centuries, read Stephen Marshall's excellent article "The Meadowlands Before the Commission: Three Centuries of Human Use and Alteration of the Newark and Hackensack Meadows," published in 2004. It can be found online at urbanhabitats.org.

3
NEW JERSEY'S WASTELAND

The history of garbage dumping in the Meadowlands spans back hundreds of years to a time when it was thought that the best way to fill the marshes for future land development was to dispose of everything that was considered waste there. Use of the Meadowlands for solid waste disposal has been extensive and undertaken with little regard for the environment or future use of the land that people thought they were reclaiming.

There wasn't a New Jersey Department of Environmental Protection or an Environmental Protection Agency (EPA) and not very many environmental laws on the books. If there were upland acres in the Meadowlands, you could rest assured it was filled with waste. In 1906, New York City garbage was used to build up the five-square-mile portion of the Meadowlands between the mouths of the Passaic and Hackensack Rivers in Kearny. That waste came in the form of household garbage, demolition from projects from surrounding towns and industrial refuse. More importantly, what was thought of as a method of land reclamation caused more harm than was then realized. No one really thought about the decomposition of the material, settlement factors, rusting materials, the generation of methane gases and the human health issues attributable to liquid and industrial wastes.

Eventually, dumping for reclamation purposes was replaced by finding the cheapest and quickest place to dump. In 1957, New York City stopped providing municipal garbage removal for commercial firms, which required companies to hire private garbage collectors. Some of these private haulers were associated with organized crime. They had "protected routes" and chose to eliminate the expense of garbage dump tipping fees by simply depositing refuse at any available location. Its highway access to the city, as well as its low population density and corresponding difficulty of identifying illegal dumpers, made the Meadowlands attractive for unregulated garbage dumps.

In 1959 alone, there were eleven major and active garbage dumps. There were no environmental laws in the state, and household garbage was under the jurisdiction of the State Department of Health. Every municipality in Bergen, Essex, Hudson, Passaic and parts of Union Counties and New York City contributed to the massive landfilling operations in the meadows. If you could truck your garbage within a relatively short run, that truck ended up in the Meadowlands. The Meadowlands contained mosquito infestations, garbage-filled open sewers and burning dumps, and some Meadowlands municipalities actually leased property to waste removal companies so they had a place to dump. Kearny, for the longest time, leased areas of its meadows to a company called Municipal Sanitary Landfill Authority (MSLA), an official-sounding organization that was nothing more than a front for a conglomerate of garbage companies under the control of various mob organizations.

The MSLA landfill operations were open every day of the year. While other dumps were closed for holidays, MSLA was always open, which at times caused problems for Newark Airport. A common characteristic of gulls in the Meadowlands is that they love fresh garbage. So the only place for gulls to go on holidays was the MSLA dumps in Kearny, which happened to be in the flight path to Newark. Thousands of gulls would swarm the site, and every time a bulldozer pushed the piles of garbage, the gulls would fly into the air and be picked up by air traffic controls at Newark Airport. It's not a good thing to see blips come and go on an air traffic controller's radar screen.

The PJP Landfill in Jersey City was owned by the Archdiocese of Newark and used by various garbage collection companies. According to a published report, the archdiocese and Edwin Seigel, the other principal owner of the area, leased the PJP Landfill tract to two men identified as Paul Capola and Philip Moscato. A spokesman for the archdiocese said in an interview that the land had never been leased by the archdiocese, adding that, "If there was any use of the land for these purposes, it was unauthorized." Although PJP was operated for many years as a landfill, the archdiocese never took any legal action against its operators.

The burning fields, which were known by the name "Brother Muscato's Dump," began accepting trash in 1969. After that, two hundred truckloads of waste, most of it in steel barrels, was deposited on the eighty-seven-acre

The Pulaski Skyway is a three-and-a-half-mile structure that crosses the Passaic and Hackensack Rivers between Newark and Jersey City. Opened in 1932, the Pulaski Skyway banned trucks in 1934. It is considered one of the most unreliable roadways in the nation. *Courtesy of the New Jersey Meadowlands Commission.*

site every day. Hazardous chemicals—such as methylene chloride, a solvent used to strip paint that is a proven cause of cancer, heart disease and central nervous system and liver issues; naphthalene, a petroleum product pesticide linked to kidney and liver damage; toluene, an industrial solvent that is toxic to the central nervous system; phenanthrene, which results from the incomplete incineration of garbage and is a suspected carcinogenic; and ethylbenzene, a solvent and diluent for paints and varnishes that may be responsible for increased incidence of tumors in the lungs, liver, kidney and testicles—were poured into the dump. The site caught fire in the early 1970s and burned for almost ten years, causing visibility problems for the Pulaski Skyway, and no one knows the extent of serious health problems that were suffered by individuals residing in the region. Ultimately, the site ended up on the Superfund List and was capped. Jimmy Hoffa's last resting stop was not under Giants stadium but Muscato's Dump.

The dump fires in the Meadowlands are vivid memories for many who lived or were brought up in the Kearny, North Arlington and Lyndhurst

The Standard Chlorine Chemical Company operated in Kearny for over ninety years, beginning in about 1903. Now a Superfund site, the entire twenty-five acres is saturated with chlorine, which is an irritant to skin, eyes and lungs. *Courtesy of the New Jersey Meadowlands Commission.*

communities. It was not uncommon to have fifty to seventy fires in Kearny alone during the 1950s and '60s. Some of the fires were caused by scavengers combing the dumps for metals that could be sold—for example, they melted the plastic coating on wire to get the copper—others were caused by spontaneous combustion or as a method to make more space for dumping.

Combinations of fog and smoke took their toll on the communities and the major highways that crossed the Meadowlands. It was a pretty common occurrence to smell the garbage burn or find soot on your car in the morning. Sometimes, the soot and ash would eat away the paint on vehicles. It was also a great concern of local fire departments that they could potentially lose a fire truck because some fires burned underground, and they never knew when the ground around the trucks would collapse. The New Jersey Turnpike section across the Meadowlands was extremely difficult to drive because of heavy smoke that combined with fog, which reduced the visibility

The obsolete Portal Bridge in Kearny that spans the Hackensack River carries Amtrak Northeast Corridor trains daily. The structure, built in 1913, swings open to allow watercraft to travel on the river. *Courtesy of the New Jersey Meadowlands Commission.*

to a few feet in front of your car or truck. In 1973, a crash on the Turnpike took nine lives and injured thirty-nine with sixty-six cars and trucks piled into one another. In the days leading up to the crash, there was a major dump fire. The fire was too hard to control, so inmates from the Rahway Correctional Facility were brought in to help by bringing the water supply to the fire, but the blaze could not be controlled. It burned out several days later.

The politics of garbage has had a significant impact on the Meadowlands district. With more than 118 municipalities dumping for years in the region, anything that could stop the use of the dumps was a major cause of distress for these towns. When the hearing for the Meadowlands legislation was held, one of the biggest concerns was the question of where the garbage was going to go. First drafts of the bill did not have the solid waste mandate in the bill. That provision was added in hopes of getting more support from legislators from Essex and Hudson. The real question remained how to manage the dumping and putting an aggressive land use plan in place. The legislative change by the sponsors put a limit on the towns that were dumping at the time the bill became law and required the commission to certify who was going to be allowed to dump. The other significant aspect of the legislation was that the commission could establish regulations on the landfills and how they operated. The bad news was the operators of those landfills were not very happy about state interference. Up until that point, they had had little or no interference from the state. This opened a whole new experience for them. Additionally, many Meadowlands towns and even Bergen County had or were going to lease more than two thousand acres of wetlands and open water to private hauling companies. Bergen County purchased the area of the Kingsland Impoundment, and Lyndhurst leased what is now the Sawmill Creek Wildlife Management Area to Viola Sanitation.

The commission hired Zurn Environmental Engineering in 1970 and gave the company the responsibility

> *to evaluate the extent and characteristics of past and existing solid waste disposal operations in the Meadowlands; to estimate the magnitude of potential solid wastes disposal operations in the Meadowlands and to examine the administrative and operational requirements associated with various regulatory situations; and to develop guidelines for regulation of solid wastes disposal operations in the Meadowlands, such that these operations might be compatible with the development of the Meadowlands and consistent with the management system.*

Zurn, with the help of the State Department of Health, conducted a survey of the waste coming into the Meadowlands. The survey found eleven active landfills and 29,469 tons per week entering those facilities. New Jersey sources contributed 25,642 tons per week, and the remaining 3,826 tons per week came from New York City area. The breakdown of the waste was one-third household, one-third industrial and one-third demolition material. The planners anticipated the life of the existing landfills would be no more than three to five years. After that time, the commission would switch to an incinerator to handle the waste, which they were required to build.

The unsung heroes in the battle to get solid waste out of the Meadowlands were the first staff members of the Meadowlands Commission—Clifford Goldman, the agency's first acting executive director, who was a protégé of Paul Ylvisaker; George Cascino, who went on to be chief engineer of the commission; and Chet Mattson, who became the director of environmental planning. They used the courts; they promulgated regulations to control the way waste was landfilled; and they used financial tools to stem the flow of garbage. The first permanent executive director—William McDowell, the former mayor of North Arlington and Bergen County freeholder, who had a mild, calm demeanor but was just as passionate as his staff—continued those policies. Anthony Scardino Jr., former state senator of District Thirty-six, which encompassed a large area of the Meadowlands, took the fight to political levels at a time when there was no more room at the landfills. He brought the fight to end garbage dumping to the halls of the statehouse.

The new commission staff addressed the dumping situation head on with restriction on landfill expansion and the policy that no wetlands or waterways were going to be used for garbage. Clifford Goldman recalls the Viola Landfill situation, in which they entered an agreement with Lyndhurst for the Sawmill area for their expansion of the Avon Landfill. They applied to the new NJDEP and the HMDC for a permit. The commission denied the permit not because of the environmental impact but because the water area was a riparian claim by the state. Viola ignored the denial and proceeded to

A crew from Weeks Marine, Incorporated, a major marine construction company, is shown removing an obsolete railroad bridge in the Kearny/Secaucus area near the New Jersey Turnpike's eastern spur. *Courtesy of the New Jersey Meadowlands Commission.*

build dikes after it received the approvals of the NJDEP. The commission sought a temporary injunction and received it from the court, only to have it reversed by the court a week later. The health emergency card of letting the garbage pile up on the streets was used then, as it would be many more times in the Meadowlands.

In the meantime, Viola started to dump in the new area only to have it collapse during a storm. The NJDEP approved a new and supplementary dike. There was a second severe storm that wiped out more of the dike structure, which resulted in the area flooding. The commission staff developed a case based on sound scientific and engineering facts. The NJDEP rescinded the permit and every other permit in the Meadowlands. Viola opted to withdraw its attempts for new a landfill and found capacity in its existing landfill for three more years.

The determination to stop the expansion of landfills continued with efforts to establish an agreement with all state agencies involved with the garbage industry to clearly define areas where garbage could or could not be dumped. The concept was to have the existing landfills continue for a specific timeframe, and instead of expanding to adjacent wetlands and waterways, the elevation of the fills would be increased. As a result, you see the garbage hills today. The garbage went up and not out. The next big test for the commission was new regulations that prohibited dumping out-of-state garbage into the Meadowlands. That challenge came to a head with the decision of the court in the *Hackensack Meadowlands Development Commission v. Municipal Sanitary Landfill Authority (MSLA)* case. MSLA, the private, mob-controlled entity, contended that the HMDC did not have the authority to promulgate such regulations and that the rule violated the intent of other laws in the state and the commerce provision of the United States Constitution. In 1975, the court ruled in favor of the commission. It was a major victory for the staff.

The landfills that were no longer active occupied about 1,500 acres, of which about 375 acres have been subsequently developed. Those past disposal operations were characterized by "dump and push" techniques followed by open burning of the deposited refuse. There was no compaction of the waste, and the burning reduced stabilization problems by virtue of destroying the organic material. Most of the development of these old sites had been commercial or warehouse uses, and it had been concentrated in the area of Route 3 and what is today Route 120 and the sports complex site. Some of these buildings suffered significant damage because of settlement. They could have made great skateboard facilities.

Of the active sites, all were found to be difficult to access in wet weather. Where the dumpsites were at the edge of wet areas, the predominant practice was to push the garbage into the water, and no daily cover was used in most cases. When cover was used, it was merely the soils surrounding the landfill, called meadow mat, that has silt characteristics.

Zurn Environmental offered several alternatives to the landfill dumping: incineration, ocean dumping, dumping in other locations using rail or composting. The company tested each alternative and determined that incineration and/or rail to other locations were the best approaches. It suggested building two or possibly three facilities in the northeast part of the district, one in Hudson County, another in Secaucus and a third in Kearny. It also suggested that the facilities be located in heavy industrial areas in order to reduce any political opposition. Unfortunately, the incinerator proposal never got going. The plan was submitted to the governor's office by 1971. The commission staff negotiated a tentative deal with Public Service Electric and Gas (PSE&G) to sell electricity generated by the incinerator. Another problem was the changing of the chairman of the commission and the dissention that occurred among the board members. The board did not yet approve the plan, but it was hoped the PSE&G agreement could move them in that direction.

The news of the incinerator reached the press, and the plan was regarded favorably until the New York City Department of Environment Protection spoke out against the project and demanded that it be blocked. The department asked the federal government to evaluate the plan because of the impact of adding to the air pollution problem in the metropolitan area. As a result, environmental groups in New Jersey opposed the incinerator. Joseph McCrane, the treasurer, held a meeting in Trenton, and before HMDC staff could start their presentation, McCrane distributed his own plan for waste disposal in the Meadowlands. It was a compacting and baling devise marketed by a Republican businessman who was thought to have a voice in the solid waste industry. The process reduced the volume of the waste, but the bales still had to be put into a landfill. (The commission eventually opened a baling facility in 1979 in North Arlington using a federal grant. It did not purchase it from the company at the McCrane meeting.) Commission staff left the meeting with the understanding that the incinerator proposal was dead. The NJDEP reviewed the plan, but the staff made it known that the report had to kill the project. The U.S. EPA also waded into the discussion and actually thought the plan could work with modifications and, in the interim, the commission should use the rail alternative.

The death of the incinerator project also was a financial setback for the commission. A twenty-five-cent-per-ton surcharge was to be placed on the waste flow. The enabling act was silent on a permanent funding source for the commission. The surcharge would have funded the agency's annual budget and would have generated enough money for the development of parks and other facilities called for in the new master plan.

A Solid Waste Management Plan

By 1976, the state passed the state Solid Waste Management Plan Act, which required each county to develop a strategy to handle the waste generated in their county. It would be more than ten years before some of the counties and their municipalities left the Meadowlands' landfills. In 1982, the Solid Waste Management Plan Act was amended to require all operating landfills in the state to have a closure date and post a plan to make sure they were closed in an environmentally safe manner and maintained in the long term. It also required the operators of the landfills to place funds in escrow to implement the closure and post-closure work. By 1981, the commission took the bold step of controlling the rates of the remaining four landfills. By then, the total amount of waste coming from Bergen, Essex, Passaic and Hudson Counties was seventy thousand tons a week. The fact that the commission took control of the dumping fees at the landfills did not sit very well with any of the private operators. To take it further, the commission required prepayment and the use of a tracking system of tons dumped. The commission staff members who were responsible for this program were exposed to the culture of the solid waste industry. Deliveries of cases of wine and scotch whiskey were sent by the haulers at Christmas as well as many other assorted gifts. The commission could have opened liquor and clothing stores. Needless to say, all of it went back with a note explaining the state's ethics code.

The culture of the garbage business also exposed the staff to individuals carrying guns and haulers making threats, but the most important thing the commission staff was taught was never be intimidated. One garbage hauler, who made the front page of the Sunday *Star-Ledger* in a story about the Genovese crime family taking over New Jersey routes, was requested and willingly complied to autograph the article. He made it clear to staff that as long as the commission treated every company equally, there would be no problems. It was the same hauler who beat up one of his drivers when he was caught at the landfill with

New York City waste. When asked about the driver, the garbage hauler said the driver fell over a leaf in his garage. The world of the landfills and the hauling companies was a world unto itself. It was always a stare down to see who was stronger and who could take another company's stops. When the commission placed itself into the financial aspects of the solid waste business to control the places where dumping could occur, staff members on the sites were threatened time and time again. Their cars were squeezed off roads, scare tactics and intimidation were tried and bulldozers came really close on the landfill.

The commission assigned garbage inspectors to physically go through suspected loads of trash to determine if they came from an approved municipality. If a company was caught bringing out-of-state waste, it was assessed a fine up to $50,000 for the infraction. The first inspector the commission hired was a gentleman known as Hoboken Jack. He was a gregarious Irishman who always had a cigar in his mouth. On his down time, he could be found at Egan's on the Belleville Turnpike and Schuyler Avenue. Jack would either be at the landfill going through garbage loads or stationed at the Holland Tunnel waiting for New York's garbage. The haulers got smart about Jack's tunnel operation and would send a "rabbit" truck for Jack to follow all the way past Newark Airport. In the meantime, they would bring their trucks from lower Manhattan to dump New York garbage illegally. One time, Jack was offered a bribe to turn the other way while trucks came in from Manhattan. When he reported the bribe offer, the New Jersey Attorney General's Office got involved, along with the state police. Hoboken Jack was fitted with a wire to record the bribe attempt. The fear was very real that Hoboken Jack might not return at the end of his shift working on the landfill. However, the person offering the bribe was arrested and brought to trial. He beat the charges and was found not guilty because the jury in Hudson County thought the accused was a victim of entrapment.

The Goodfellas

The people who had to be watched closely were the field inspectors, weigh masters and checkers employed by the commission who were constantly tested by haulers to either look the other way or make a "mistake" on the weight of the truck. Several times, the state police were called in if there was a problem or someone was suspected of being on the take. Throughout the operation, undercover state police tested the systems and the employees. A sure sign in the solid waste industry that something was wrong was when a driver would pass his pornographic magazine to a checker or weigh master. More times than not, the place markers inside were hundred dollar bills. Schuyler Avenue was a great location for the state police to look down on the landfills to see all of the activity. There were several cases where insurance or salvage companies dumped electronics, wine, liquor, sunglasses or any products that were damaged in transport from either Port Newark or Elizabeth to warehouses. The companies would bring the damaged products for disposal by dumping in one of the landfills. If the load was actually in good shape, the bulldozer operator would bury it in the landfill, wait until the insurance company people were gone and very gingerly remove the covering layer and recover the goods.

The Politics of Garbage Disposal

The commission had to find an environmentally safe way to close landfills that were active prior to 1982. Because it was not going to get help from Trenton on implementing the solid waste management plan that forced counties to accept the mandate of handling their own waste, the commission took over the responsibility of these landfills and opened them for short periods of time to generate enough money to close them properly. The commission called these landfills "orphan landfills" because they lacked the funds to address the environmental impacts they were causing. The commission collected over $140 million to install cutoff walls and French drainage systems behind the wall to carry off the rainwater that percolates through the landfills, which is also called leachate. The system prevents contaminates from entering the surrounding wetlands and waterways. A cap was put on the site and methane gas recovered. At one time, the methane was used to generate electricity.

Unfortunately, the fund became a source of great income for the state. It was available anytime the state had a large deficit or needed funding for another program. Beginning with the Whitman administration, the fund was tapped to pay for security for the World Cup held in the Meadowlands. All of the police departments that paid overtime or bought new equipment for World Cup security were reimbursed. The total cost was $4 million. The $4 million contribution stayed in the state budget until it was decided to use the fund as part of the proposed EnCap project to pay off the stranded debt of Bergen County. The balance of the fund was used a couple of years later by the state to balance the budget during the McGreevey administration. The $140 million was lost forever. The attorney general's office had to write an opinion letter to the auditors of the commission that the responsibility of closure and post closure was now the responsibility of the state. Without that letter, the commission would have received a qualified opinion because of the large unfunded liability. If the commission received that opinion, the state would have also received that opinion. The rule was learned—never plan ahead and collect cash upfront for a thirty-year liability because the state will take it.

Garbage disposal equaled political pressure on the towns and counties. Commission meetings were filled with freeholders: legislators asking for another year, several months or even several weeks for dumping. They told the stories of how garbage would be stacked on the street and the smell and disease would create a health emergency. Members of the Essex County delegation introduced legislation to require the commission to find space for the county's garbage. The commission staff was called to Trenton for a meeting with the NJDEP commissioner, and the county executive of Hudson County asked that the commission be required to take their garbage. Essex and Passaic Counties municipalities and, in particular, the City of Newark fought long and hard in court to force the commission to find them new space. The court cases were based on the language in the enabling act that required the commission to handle the waste documented in 1969. Eventually, that was true for every county and town that dumped in the district. In some cases, the commission made financial settlements, some as high as $12 million, to assist the counties with their planning efforts just to get them out of the Meadowlands. Bergen County was the last to use the Lyndhurst landfill for household garbage. It was politically easier and strategic for administrations in Trenton to side with the counties as opposed to a state agency under their control.

Green Lands Replace Garbage Dumps

The commission had planned a two-thousand-acre park from Lyndhurst to Kearny. The DeKorte Park (NJDEP refused to call it a state park) was named after Assemblyman Richard DeKorte. DeKorte was elected to the New Jersey General Assembly in 1967 and was later elected majority leader with Thomas Kean as Speaker. He was one of the instrumental figures who helped push through the Meadowlands Act. In 1970, DeKorte was appointed counsel to Governor William T. Cahill. When Cahill lost his primary election and Brendan Byrne was elected governor, he was so impressed with the DeKorte that he made him director of the new State Energy Office. Richard DeKorte passed away in 1975.

The commission, with its garbage baler up and running, created cubes that were stacked in layers rather than dumped. Staff members surveyed the entire site and created contours for the park. There were to be boating lakes, camping areas and a commercial/residential development on the old Erie Landfill in North Arlington. With the political pressure mounting and NJDEP siding with some of the counties to continue dumping, the contouring ended. The potential rolling hills were filled and went higher and higher to give more time to the counties. The rolling hills of what was going to be a recreational area became a mountain 150 feet high, flat across the top and stretched across old landfills from Kearny to North Arlington between Turnpike Exits 15 West and 16 West. The area that was to be a boating lake was actually drained and excavated down 30 feet and backfilled with Bergen County garbage.

Artist Nancy Holt presented a proposal to the commission for the development of a modern Stonehenge on top of one of the landfills in Kearny. It would have steel rods aligned with stars at different times of year; small, cave-like structures to view planets; and a structure for the establishment of an observatory for viewing the planets and stars. That concept would come in at a price tag of almost $500,000. The project received significant press coverage. Several factors were not taken into consideration. Every landfill, especially a dumpsite with organics in the waste, will decompose, and in that process, methane gas is generated. As garbage decomposes, the landfill settles, and the elevation drops and could drop quite a bit over a period of time. With that combination, the alignment for planet gazing would require a tremendous amount of maintenance. Needless to say, the project was abandoned.

By the mid-1980s, the landfills in Kearny and North Arlington were seeing the end of their capacity. The counties and municipalities that dumped seventy thousand tons of garbage every week were relegated to using transfer stations at quadruple the Meadowlands dumping rates to ship their waste out of state. The political power of garbage slowed the commission's efforts to move forward with a development plan.

The Blue Claw Crabs by Dr. Angela Cristini

The blue crab (*Callinectes sapidus*), also known as the blue claw crab, is so named because of the bright blue color of the surface of its two large claws that face toward the body of the animal. Females can be identified right away because they have red-tipped claws—people like to say they are wearing "nail polish."

This species has a wide distribution in the bays and estuaries along the Atlantic coast of the United States from the south shore of Cape Cod to the southern tip of Florida. Blue claws also live in the Gulf of Mexico—from Florida to Texas.

The first crabbers in the Hackensack and Newark Bay region—Native Americans, followed by Europeans—used these abundant, pugnacious crustaceans as a source of food. Extraction of crabs for local consumption and for sale was increased in the Hackensack River as the salt water from Newark Bay moved farther up the river because various engineering projects, starting as early as the 1820s, reduced the flow of fresh water downstream.

The saltier river/estuary is the perfect habitat for this animal, which scavenges for a living; lots of small fish, soft-shelled and young cherrystone

A large blue claw crab collected in a Meadowlands estuary. Shellfish from this river system should not be consumed under any circumstances. *Courtesy of the New Jersey Meadowlands Commission.*

clams, marine worms, the remains of larger fish, turtles and anything that has died in the water serve as food. Blue claws, being crustaceans, have their skeletons on the outside of their bodies; this "armor" and their formidable claws make them almost invincible as adults. They are vulnerable when they shed their shells to grow (molting). We know them in this stage as "soft-shells," and they are a very valuable part of the commercial crab industry in the United States. People, larger fish and birds love soft-shelled crabs. Juvenile crabs are an important food for fish, birds and diamondback terrapins in the Hackensack River. Their position as scavengers and their importance to the trophic structure makes *Callinectes* a critically important part of this ecosystem.

From the early 1800s through the twentieth century, a wide variety of chemicals was introduced into the Hackensack River system. One of the most toxic in this cocktail is Dioxin 2, 3, 7, 8—*tetrachlorodibenzo para dioxin (TCDD)*. There are 419 types of dioxin related compounds and 30 have toxicity, with TCDD being the most toxic. Dioxins belong to the "dirty dozen" of dangerous, persistent, organic pollutants. They all:

- Have potential to affect a number of organs and systems
- Are chemically stable and absorbed and stored by fat
- Have a half-life in the body of seven to eleven years
- Accumulate in the aquatic food chain

Dioxin is found in the mud in Newark Bay because of pollution from a chemical company (Diamond Alkali) that manufactured herbicides in the 1960s. The entire area and the section of the Passaic River adjacent to Diamond Alkali is a Federal Superfund site.

Dioxin gets into crabs by trophic transfer from sediments to crab food. Crabs eat the critters that ingest contaminated mud (clams, worms, shrimp and some fish). Some of the fine mud containing dioxin has been moved up into the Hackensack from Newark Bay by the motion of the tides, but it is likely that most of the accumulation of chemicals like dioxin results from movement of the crabs foraging for food throughout the system during their life cycle.

A basic understanding of what is meant by numbers used in describing concentrations of pollutants helps in order to understand more about the contamination problem. One part per hundred (percent) is 1 percent. One part per billion, abbreviated ppb, (one sheet in a roll of toilet paper from New York to London) is the concentration range of PCBs in seafood that can cause health effects when eaten by humans. One part per trillion, abbreviated ppt, (one drop of detergent in enough water to fill a string of railroad cars ten miles long) is the concentration range of dioxins in seafood that can cause health effects when eaten by humans. The warning level for safe consumption is twenty-five ppt for dioxin.

We have conducted a study aimed at determining how much dioxin was accumulating in crabs from the Newark Bay system that were big enough for people to eat. The results indicated that dioxin accumulates in adult crabs in this system above the level for safe consumption and are a health hazard for people who eat crabs. The following are effects of dioxins on human health:

- Short-term: skin lesions, chloracne, darkening of the skin and altered liver function
- Long-term: impairment of immune system, developing nervous system, endocrine system and reproductive functions
- Chronic exposure of animals to dioxins has resulted in several types of cancer. WHO classified TCDD as a "known human carcinogen"

In a public announcement on July 15, 2014, the NJDEP, in partnership with the New Jersey Department of Health, municipal governments and local environmental organizations, again warned anglers and the public not to harvest or consume blue claw crabs from the Lower Passaic River, Newark Bay and surrounding waters, including the Hackensack River. "Crabs in these waters are abundant and appear healthy but they are not safe to eat," said NJDEP commissioner Bob Martin. "We have to be vigilant about preventing people from eating crabs caught in these waters because they can be harmful to those who consume them, especially vulnerable populations…In concert with the federal government, we are now working to develop a massive cleanup project that will make these waterways safe for generations in the future, but the warnings remain in effect now."

As they have for years, the NJDEP and DOH are working with local municipalities to distribute informative literature and signs about the crab consumption ban and fish consumption advisories. Signs and literature are available in English, Spanish, Polish, Portuguese, Cantonese, Korean and Tagalog to make this information as accessible as possible. Signs are located in places frequented by the public, especially those areas where there is evidence of crabbing activity. The signs warn of the crabs' toxicity as well as the legal repercussions associated with harvesting them.

Dr. Angela Cristini is the director of the Meadowlands Environment Center, professor of biology and assistant vice-president for grants and sponsored programs at Ramapo College of New Jersey. She is a nationally recognized authority on Callinectes sapidus *and other marine species.*

4
THE NEW MEADOWLANDS

Running parallel to addressing the solid waste problem, a master plan was introduced in 1970. The final adoption occurred in 1972. The plan was critical in convincing people the next great planning and land use experiment was not another plan doomed for failure. When looking at the Meadowland enabling act, it is clear to see that the scope and number of tools given to the commission and the authority and power behind its land use authority were amazing and very unlikely to happen again. To make sure the garbage would never replace development opportunities, every inch of the region was given a land use.

Picture the political landscape for the commission from the time the master plan was introduced in 1970 to its final adoption in 1972. Add to the equation land use regulations adopted in 1972 that were guidelines for the development of the master plan. The commission was dealing with the solid waste issue with the thought that a new technology and approach of disposal was coming on line, mayors that were still fighting the constitutionality of the agency and its tax sharing concept, property owners refusing to acknowledge the authority of the master plan, a change in governor from Hughes to Cahill and the creation the New Jersey Sports and Exposition Authority that carved out 750 acres in the heart of the Meadowlands district that the commission had no control over. The Transcontinental Gas Company decided it was going to build natural gas storage tanks in Carlstadt in an area that was designated for housing. The commission went to court and lost because the company was covered under the interstate commerce clause and is considered a utility under the Federal

Giants Stadium under construction in November 1975. Route 3 is in the photo's center, and the New Jersey Turnpike is at the bottom right. *New Jersey Sports and Exhibition Authority.*

Energy Regulatory Authority (FERC). A new chairman of the commission was appointed: Lawrence Kramer, Department of Community Affairs commissioner and former mayor of the city of Paterson. A new permanent executive director, William McDowell, was also chosen. It was a daunting task to put a plan together that would work and change the identity of the area forever. The Cahill administration did not make it easy for the commission staff. The commission, which Hughes and Ylivasker envisioned being the force behind development for the region, was relegated to the role of a facilitator.

A DEVELOPMENT PLAN

The commission hired Dan Coleman Associates from Chicago to undertake the development of the plan. The small commission staff worked with Coleman and surveyed every aspect of the district. The staff determined where each element of development should begin. George Cascino, former chief engineer of the HMDC, recalls the painstaking efforts in putting the plan together and the obstacles faced to complete the plan as quickly as possible. He also remembers having a transportation engineer intern assisting on the project that lobbied long and hard about where a major mass transit hub should be. His name was Rich Roberts. Roberts insisted that Coleman Associates was wrong when it placed the transit hub in Kearny. He pointed out that there was a place in Secaucus where many of the rail lines in northern New Jersey came together so passengers could get to New York City and Penn Station in Newark. He pointed to the area in Secaucus near the Jersey City border. Roberts prevailed, and the location he chose is where we now have the Lautenberg Station, and Rich Roberts is now the chief planner at New Jersey Transit.

The Master Plan

When the draft came out in 1970, the plan called for the following: seventy thousand residential units, three million square feet of commercial space, twenty million square feet of office space, ninety million square feet of industrial and warehouse space and ten thousand hotel rooms. The plan broke the district into six major land use categories: employment areas, which included warehouse distribution, a research park and a manufacturing area; business districts, which included a regional retail mall and a residential, office and entertainment center called Berry's Creek Center; commercial areas, including hotels, office buildings and highway commercial and neighborhood shopping centers; public uses, which included a cultural center, a transportation center and other special uses; educational facilities for high school and elementary schools; and recreational areas like public parks, recreational facilities and residential areas that built housing on cluster islands close to parks and open space areas. The residential component called for 180,000 thousand people to live in the Meadowlands. The plan included 2,600 acres of wetlands to be filled to meet the master plan goals.

The ambitious plan did not take into consideration the environmental aspects of such a large amount of development. When the master plan was introduced, there were two schools of thought about what the plan should be. The environmentalist who spoke up on the bill took a position that the Meadowlands should not be developed to the extent that the plan outlined. They preferred open space, parks and the protection of marshland areas. It was

Allied Junction, a fanciful design surrounding what is now called the Lautenberg Rail Station. The 2003 proposal called for 700,000 square feet of shopping, a four-hundred-room hotel and a twenty-five-story glass tower. *Courtesy of the New Jersey Meadowlands Commission.*

thought that the Meadowlands Commission and its new power could create open space at will without consideration of landowners being compensated and the impact on riparian claims. It was at a time when no one knew how to handle the riparian issue. Did the commission have to pay those claims or was the state willing to give the properties and disregard the School Fund? In addition to fighting the solid waste issue, the commission looked to avoid claims of inverse condemnation or a "takings" case; they gave a land use designation to every piece of property—wetlands, landfills and uplands.

The landowners wanted to see the maximum development possible. The plan would have a very positive impact on their land values. The cities surrounding the Meadowlands were concerned about the amount of office space in the master plan because of their redevelopment efforts and did not want a further exodus of the middle class that occurred after the 1967 Newark riots. The municipalities did not want housing that would have an impact on their schools and municipal services. They preferred a plan that was based on industrial and warehouse uses. It is the same debate that goes on even today in the Meadowlands and in most municipalities in the state.

At the public hearings held in Bergen and Hudson Counties, the commission received testimony from many environmental groups; planning organizations; local municipal officials, including superintendents of school districts; and landowners. Everyone had very specific interests, and to summarize the comments, the plan was harmful to the environment from an air quality stance, there was too much development, not enough development, too many wetlands were being impacted, the plan was excellent (from property owners who had high-density zoning), there was no room for new students from the developments in the schools, the permitting process was too cumbersome, the permitting process was too easy, the fact that in certain zones you needed 80 percent of the owners of the properties to agree on a plan would stop development, the solid waste problem was not solved, there was no sewer capacity and there was not enough transportation capacity. The pros and cons of development and the effect on the environment that were spelled out in those hearings are the same that you hear today.

The NJDEP decided to do an environmental impact statement on the plan and asked the HMDC to delay the final adoption of the master plan. It covered water pollution, air pollution and marsh conservation. It did not cover the impacts of the solid waste disposal. The NJDEP helped finance a feasibility study regarding sewer treatment in the Meadowlands, and it reviewed three plans that included a combination of the three. The NJDEP decided it was best to go with a plan whereby everything east of the Hackensack River would go to Hudson County and everything west to Bergen County. The proposal for the commission to handle sewer treatment was rejected. This was another obstacle for the commission.

The NJDEP found the district contained 6,877 acres of wetland. Of these wetlands, the district rated 3,100 acres, or 52.36 percent of the total acreage, of high ecological value. Wetlands that were rated moderately functioning wetlands accounted for 1,403 acres, or 20.40 percent, and the low-value wetlands totaled 2,374 acres, or 27.24 percent. The district recommended further study of the wetlands and that the commission should incorporate the NJDEP "Wetlands Order" into the zoning regulations. All high-value wetlands should be preserved.

The HMDC's performance standards of the regulations were found to be equal to or more stringent than the state's. The performance standards reviewed were for water quality, air pollution, noise, vibrations, radiation, light sources, herbicides and pesticides.

The Regional Plan Association (RPA) voiced its opinion regarding the development in the Meadowlands, especially how it would impact the urban centers around the Meadowlands region. The RPA had been critical of the master plan on several points. It said the Meadowlands plan would take office development from the cities and thus cause the further demise of urban centers and erode job production. The association also pointed out that the commission's plan would be taking away the opportunity for better housing in the cities and that additional open space was lacking. The RPA was viewed not as a New Jersey organization but as the tool of the City of New York funded and organized by major corporations with their headquarters in the city. Regardless, the RPA was viewed as an influential organization that should be acknowledged, and it was, by Chairman Kramer, former mayor of Paterson.

Tax Sharing

Another major issue that came up during this period was the need to make changes in the enabling act that affected the tax sharing formula and several other provisions of the act. The changes were a result of the issue of the constitutionality of the act that made its way up to the New Jersey Supreme Court. The first hearing before the court occurred in February 1972. The amendments corrected provisions on how the inter-municipal tax sharing formula was calculated for each town. The language in the enabling legislation would give the commission the direct power to make assessments and levy taxes, which would have been unconstitutional.

Inter-municipal tax sharing is best described by the New Jersey Meadowlands Commission as

> *the need to create a fiscal device to share the benefits of development as they zoned certain areas for industrial, commercial and residential use and others for parks, highways, open space and other non-taxable public uses. The Master Plan was created on the basis of the best possible use of land based on its location and needs. In approaching zoning on a regional basis, the possibility of financial inequities arose. Simply stated, if a large section of Community A is zoned for a park and a large section of Community B is zoned for a major office, residential or warehouse project, then Community B should share some of the benefits derived from development. The tax*

> *sharing plan was designed to balance these inequities so that the region could be developed as a unit with town-to-town equality. In short, each community will get a proportionate share of the property taxes from "new" (post 1970) development, regardless of where it occurs.*

There were several other changes made, including eliminating a credit to municipalities as a result of daytime work population and contributions into an infrastructure fund. The language dealing with riparian title claims was also removed. In the initial act, the commission was given authority to satisfy riparian claims.

The commission adopted the modified master plan in November 1972. The modifications to the plan included downward adjustments to the number of the housing units, office space and increased the amount of open space. The development of the Meadowlands was on its way.

5

THE GREAT EXPERIMENT

Hartz Mountain's Harmon Cove

In 1969, full-page advertisements began to appear in the Sunday *New York Times* real estate section. They featured an artist's sketch of wood-clad town homes along with seagulls perched on pilings next to a wood dock. The ad appeared at first glance to be for a new development on Cape Cod or some other beachfront community. A closer inspection revealed that the condominiums were under development in a place called Harmon Cove, which was somewhere in New Jersey. Driving instructions were included in the ad's small type near the bottom of the page, but there wasn't a hint that the development was located in the small town of Secaucus, which had a notorious reputation due to the decades of livestock farming within its boundaries. The project was the second real estate venture for the Hartz Mountain pet products company, the leaders in the manufacturing and distribution of pet foods and pet supplies packaged in the familiar orange boxes found in all food markets and variety stores.

The Hartz Mountain Company began in 1926 when the German Jewish entrepreneur Max Stern and his brother, Gustiv, arrived in New York City after traveling on the Hamburg American Steamship Line from Germany accompanying five thousand canaries. The birds were quickly sold to the John Wanamaker Department Store on Astor Place in Manhattan. Wanamaker's had begun in Philadelphia in 1876 and was so successful that a New York branch store opened soon after. John Wanamaker was an enlightened businessman whose employees were provided with recreational activities, free medical care, profit sharing and pensions. The Philadelphia store was modeled after the great

A section of Harmon Cove showing two phases of town homes and the Panasonic campus on the right. *Courtesy of the Meadowlands Regional Chamber of Commerce.*

retail emporiums of Europe and was the first department store with electric lights and a telephone. The canaries sold quickly as Americans fell in love with the handsome yellow songbird that was easy to keep and inexpensive to purchase. Max Stern made many trips back to Germany prior to the period that preceded World War II in order to purchase more canaries, which he quickly sold to the giant retailers of the time, including Macys, Woolworth's, W.T. Grant and S.S. Kresge, the forerunner of K-Mart.

The Sterns purchased a building not far from Wannamaker's New York Store and began to produce birdseed and, eventually, a full range of pet products, many of which were made available for the first time commercially. In 1959, Max's son, Leonard, joined the business, and he believed that the great success in supplying products for birds' care and feeding could be expanded to include products for all kinds of house pets and domesticated animals. Soon the Hartz Mountain brand was the most recognizable line of pet products in the nation.

In 1966, Leonard Stern was ready to move beyond pet products. He seized on an opportunity to develop a 700,000-square-foot warehousing facility in Bayonne, New Jersey. Because of the proximity to the whole of New York City, Long Island, Southern New England and Philadelphia, New Jersey is ideal for warehousing the millions of products that are imported to or exported from the northeastern United States. The Eisenhower Interstate Highway System authorized in 1956 had begun to join highways from one state to another, making commercial trucking and warehousing a new-growth industry. Stern's Bayonne facility met an immediate demand for large, safe, clean temporary storage space near the Port of New York and New Jersey, the expanded Newark Airport and the New Jersey Turnpike (Interstate 95), a segment of the Interstate Highway System. Happy with the success in Bayonne, Leonard sought out other real estate projects in New Jersey and discovered that in an overlooked and undeveloped area near New York City, it was possible to acquire tracts of land at reasonable cost.

Harmon Cove Begins

He discovered an underdeveloped place in an area known locally as the Hackensack Meadowlands. Actually located in the town of Secaucus, the two tracts of land bordered the former noxious pig farms that had kept the village from prospering. Hartz Mountain purchased the 1,250 acres for about $8,000 an acre and began the project that changed the Meadowlands forever. The project, known as Harmon Cove, was risky and audacious, but the Sterns correctly surmised that first-class commercial, residential and warehousing space six miles from Midtown Manhattan was desirable on many levels. The original developments used some wetlands that would have been preserved today, but at the time, the practice wasn't illegal or even unusual.

The project began with the building of manufacturing and warehousing facilities. By this time, property in Manhattan was too valuable to use for either activity as residential buildings were under construction in many parts of Manhattan that were not traditionally housing sections of the city. Lofts all over Manhattan that had formerly been used for manufacturing were now legally available for residential use for the first time. Manufacturing and storage was leaving, and Secaucus was fifteen minutes from the Manhattan entrance to the Lincoln Tunnel.

Harmon Cove began to take shape with a broad boulevard in its center. At the northern end near the new Meadowlands parkway under construction, the Sterns accomplished perhaps their greatest triumph by convincing Japan's Matsushta Electronic Company to establish its North American headquarters for its Panasonic brand in the Meadowlands. In the 1970s, Panasonic's forty-acre campus containing 941,000 square feet of warehouse and office space was a showplace for foreign industrial corporations operating in America. At that time, Bergen County, New Jersey, was the home of so many Japanese corporations that high schools offered courses in Japanese language and colleges offered English language and American culture programs for the wives of Japanese executives residing in the county. Most of the Japanese companies have scaled down their presence in Bergen County or have left the area, including Panasonic, which moved to Newark in 2013. The State of New Jersey provided a tax credit to Panasonic in the amount of $102 million to move to a location in Newark about twenty miles away. The Sterns and the Town of Secaucus protested the state's encouragement of the move to Newark claiming that the tax incentive was intended only to entice companies from out of state to move their operations to New Jersey not to steal a company from a New Jersey town and locate it in another place in the state.

Close to the Panasonic campus, the Sterns engaged in their first residential real estate activity. Harmon Cove I was built along the Hackensack River and featured a marina for small boats owned by the new residents of the natural wood–sheaved condominium units. The town houses were spacious and well appointed with assigned parking on the ground level. Harmon Cove II, built back from the river, offered even larger town house units and was landscaped with cherry trees planted throughout the development. It was easy to forget that the Harmon Cove residences were built on the former livestock farmland that had plagued the town, and later a section of the New Jersey Turnpike, for decades. The next residential project was a high-rise condominium complex about one mile from the town houses that had a rocky beginning because the residential real estate market had softened. Presently, all of the Harmon Cove town houses and flats enjoy high resale value. Along with living quarters, the Sterns built the region's first outlet center, attracting famous brands of apparel, which in turn attracted buyers from New York City, Upstate New York and southern New England as well as people from all over New Jersey.

Food markets, restaurants and service businesses moved into the Stern's retail buildings and commercial tenants into premier offices in their office buildings, which eventually numbered one thousand. Schools, parks and a hospital were built for the growing community. Hartz Mountain Industries was the engine that moved the entire Meadowlands region from a forgotten marsh crossed by the turnpike into a dynamic piece of the New York Metropolitan Area where careers and opportunities became available for countless numbers of individuals. Other builders developed commercial and residential projects in Lyndhurst and the Newport section of Jersey City using the Harmon Cove model. The Sterns continued to dream by building in Weehawken, Ridgefield Park, the Jersey City waterfront, Newark, Manhattan and throughout America but remained based in Secaucus in one of their own finely landscaped buildings in the heart of the Meadowlands.

Just before the adoption of the Meadowlands Act, Leonard Stern purchased open land in Secaucus for $10 million. It was Hartz Mountain Industries' largest purchase of real estate, accomplished at a time when the land was universally viewed to be too difficult to build on and too risky for an investment. The area nearest to the Hackensack River had been filled with dredge material from the river since 1931 when a seaplane facility was going to be built. Hartz purchased more than one thousand acres of land from interests that included Eugene Mori, who had sought to open a racetrack, and property that was once owned by Curtiss Wright Aviation that had been part of the plan for an airport and seaplane facility. When the Meadowlands Act went into effect, Leonard Stern thought he had made the biggest mistake of his life. He was not sure what the ramifications of the new law would be on the property he had just purchased. Stern believed that he would be able to build a complex of warehouses that could serve the New York/New Jersey metropolitan area. The mayor of Secaucus was Paul Amico, who became the full-time mayor after selling his two successful diner businesses along what is now Route 3. Paul's Diner was the place to go for good coffee and food. Mayor Amico lived his entire life in Secaucus and went to school only up to the fifth grade. Amico, who is approaching his 102nd birthday, recalls his first meeting with Gene Heller, executive vice-president of Hartz, begging the mayor to find the political means to move the Meadowland Commission boundary line so the Hartz properties were not included in the district. The mayor was sympathetic, and through Assemblyman Guarini's support, the boundary was altered so the center of town was removed from the district. The mayor requested the boundary move because that part of Secaucus was already developed with its own central business district and it was where most of the town's people lived. In essence, 100 percent of Secaucus was in the district and under the jurisdiction of the Meadowlands. The mayor expended his political capital on the first change and was not going take a chance to move the line again.

When the Hartz people first met with the commission to discuss potential land uses, their first plan was for warehousing. George Cascino, the chief engineer and a member of the staff who worked on the new master plan, made it very clear that warehousing could go on some of the properties, but the area closest to the river on the master plan was designed for housing. The commission staff, after the issuance of the interim master plan and eventual adoption of the document, received many applications for development, some of which met the plan and many that did not. The staff correctly refused to deviate from what the vision document contained.

Cascino suggested to Hartz it look at the development of Sausalito, a California city near the San Francisco Bay Area. To Hartz's credit, it did just that and came back with a mixed-use residential development along the Hackensack River. That forward-looking vision and determination was a huge success story going forward. The company's application was submitted to the HMDC in 1973 for the Specially Planned Area known as Island Residential 1 (IR-1) Zone. The application was for 257 acres along the river and called for the following: 626 town house residential units, an office and commercial complex, a hospital, a ten-story office building, a movie theater, a hotel, professional office buildings, a racquet club, parklands, parking structures and warehouses. The commission approved the application in September 1974.

When Hartz started construction of the town houses, the first models built were one-, two- and three-bedroom units. The price for the one bedroom was $39,000, the two bedrooms were $49,000 and the three bedrooms were

Marking the investment of $1 billion in 1981 of new projects in the Meadowlands district. *From left to right*: Anthony Scardino Jr., John Renna, Jon Hansen, Governor Tom Kean, Gene Heller and Leonard Stern. *Courtesy of the Meadowlands Regional Chamber of Commerce.*

$69,000. A trip to the site caused a first blush reaction, "Why would I want to live here?"

Once the first phase of Harmon Cove was underway and several components were built or close to completion; Hartz submitted to the commission its next phases of development, which included mid-rise and high-rise developments. The idea of a high-rise coming to Secaucus caused a political firestorm in the community. Even Anthony Imperiale, a state senator at the time, came to voice his opinion in favor of an organization that opposed the development, the Secaucus Citizens Opposing High Rises (SCOHR). The commission downsized the project to only 1,480 condo units.

Stern's analysis proved true, as Harmon Cove evolved into a premier real estate development. Harmon Cove was Hartz Mountain's first mixed-use community and, at one time, contained more than thirteen million square feet of warehouse and distribution facilities and office space, 120 outlet stores, three hotels, 1,400 luxury condominium apartments in the Harmon Cove Towers and town house condominiums in two side-by-side Hackensack River

A warehouse near the headquarters of Goya Foods in Secaucus. The company, founded in 1936, is the largest Hispanic-owned food products company in the United States. *Courtesy of the Meadowlands Regional Chamber of Commerce.*

waterfront developments. The many innovations at Harmon Cove include not just the development of state-of-the-art industrial, office and residential properties. The outlet mall concept was also pioneered at Harmon Cove, and it has become a place where people can live, work, shop and stay. Harmon Cove was the first of many innovative threshold projects Hartz brought to North Jersey and the broader metropolitan area.

Hartz Mountain Industries has renovated or demolished some of its original buildings in the Meadowlands. It is presently building more residential than commercial spaces as the market for office space in the region has softened, but the demand for living quarters close to New York City has risen due to the very high cost of residential space in Manhattan, Brooklyn and Queens. In 1997, Emanuel Stern, the third generation of Sterns, became president and chief operating officer of Hartz Mountain Industries. Soon after, his brother, Edward Stern, founded Hartz Capital, the investment arm of the Hartz group that invests in new technology and emerging industries. Leonard Stern's great experiment in the Meadowlands was spectacularly successful. His legacy is a permanent economic system enriched and expanded by Emanuel Stern. Market change has impacted the great Meadowlands marsh and the surrounding region only in positive ways.

6
MUSIC IN THE MEADOWLANDS

New Jersey can rightfully call itself the "Music State" rather the "Garden State," which almost no one understands. Residents of the state are used to seeing and hearing the best offerings of popular music written, arranged and performed by super-talented New Jersey natives along with other brilliant international performers. The places that have hosted New Jersey's finest music makers are a list of historic music halls, some of which have survived and some of which have closed.

Asbury Park's Italianate Paramount Theater was opened in 1930, and the 1,600-seat venue has hosted motion pictures, plays and, of course, concerts. Throughout the theater's eighty-year history, its future was always in doubt as populations shifted, and Asbury Park experienced a drop in its popularity. The Paramount struggled for decades after single-screen movie houses became unprofitable. At one time, six theaters offered newly released films in Asbury Park. All are gone except the Paramount, which was placed on the National Register for Historic Places in 1979, providing some protection against its destruction.

In Red Bank, the storied Carlton Theater, which opened in 1926, had a similar history, but the building that is considered "an architectural triumph and a marvel of beauty" has attracted strong artistic support since the 1970s. Performances by music legends Tony Bennett, Martha Graham, Rosemary Clooney, James Brown and Grover Washington Jr. set the standard. On the most memorable evening in the theater's history, May 11, 1979, "The Kid from Red Bank," the town's favorite son, Count Basie with his orchestra performed for an AME Zion church building drive. The Carlton was renamed the Count Basie Theater in 1984 in tribute to the great music man.

New Brunswick's State Theater was designed by Thomas W. Lamb, the leading theater architect of the Roaring Twenties, an era in which magnificent vaudeville and silent film palaces were opened throughout the nation. The State Theater, like most other movie houses, suffered a decline in the 1960s and closed. In 1987, after being acquired by a not-for-profit cultural organization, the State Theater reopened and attracted major performers due to its excellent visual seating plan and fine acoustics. The audiences returned, and in 2003, a complete restoration of the classic theater was undertaken.

Passaic's Capitol Theater opened as a vaudeville house and later was transformed into a movie theater. The 3,200-seat theater fell on hard times in the 1960s but was rescued by concert promoter John Scher, who brought a dizzying collection of rock-and-roll bands to the Capitol. For a decade and a half, Scher presented the performances of true music legends to appreciative audiences. Before being demolished in 1991, the Capitol offered the sounds of the Byrds, Billy Joel, the Grateful Dead, the Four Seasons, the Who, the Rolling Stones, Van Morrison, Bruce Springsteen and the E Street Band and the Allman Brothers Band. A list of performers on this level will never again be duplicated in a relatively small venue, because by the mid-1980s, world-class concerts had to be offered at much larger places in order to be profitable. Considering that New Jersey is the nation's most densely populated state and that the creation and performance of music is a part of the state's DNA, it's odd that, until the opening of the Byrne Arena in the Meadowlands in 1981, no large stage for musical performance existed.

It was almost accidental, certainly incidental, that the new arena rising in the open space across from Giants Stadium in the Meadowlands could also be used as a concert venue with seating for twenty thousand. Work on the Brendan Byrne Arena began in 1977, and the facility opened in 1981 as the home of the New York Nets basketball team, which had moved from Long Island. The team played in the Byrne Arena, later called the Continental and now the Izod Arena, until 2010 when it moved to the Prudential Center in Newark for two seasons and then to the Barclays Center in Brooklyn. Built as a basketball arena, the Byrne/Izod has hosted two decades of NBA play, countless tournaments, college basketball and All-Star Games, but there is a back story regarding its original purpose.

Hockey was a growing national sport in the 1970s, and a group of business people associated with then governor Brendan Byrne desired to bring to the Garden State a hockey team, which would be known as a New Jersey team and not a transplanted New York team operating across the Hudson River.

The signing of the act authorizing the building of the Byrne Arena on January 2, 1979. *Seated, from left to right*: Alfred Linkletter, Governor Brenden Byrne, William Hyland and Eugene Dinallo. *Standing, from left to right*: Clifford Goldman, Aubrey Lewis and Gerald Breslin. *New Jersey Sports and Exhibition Authority.*

Entrepreneur Arthur Imperatore, who was long associated with pioneering businesses in northern New Jersey, acquired the Colorado Rockies hockey team that played out of Denver. The National Hockey League (NHL) rejected the plan to move the Rockies to New Jersey as there wasn't an arena in the state that met NHL standards. Eventually, the Byrne Arena was finished, and the team was relocated to the Meadowlands in 1982. Its name was changed to the New Jersey Devils. The Devils stayed in the Meadowlands until 2007 and relocated to Newark's Prudential Center for the 2008 season.

Sometime during the design phase, the architects were reminded that music was one of the state's most important products, and no place in New Jersey was there a first-class concert space large enough to host the great performers. The arena's design was amended to include concert hall acoustics fine enough to satisfy the world's top bands and their sound experts and a good view of the stage from every seat. In fact, while the arena was consistently ranked as the worst NBA home court in the league,

Construction was beginning at the Byrne Arena site (top right) adjacent to Giants Stadium in 1979. *New Jersey Sports and Exhibition Authority.*

it is recognized for the high-quality music reproduction that emerges in a space built primarily for witnessing basketball and hockey, not for listening to the mellow sound of Frank Sinatra and the exciting performances of Bruce Springsteen and the E Street Band.

In July 1981, the Byrne Arena opened officially with a series of six concerts by Bruce Springsteen. Nicknamed "Boss," Springsteen—a Freehold, New Jersey native—is among the best known rock-and-roll composers and performers in the world. Springsteen and the accompanying musicians who eventually were named the E Street Band have appeared eight times in the Meadowlands, including the record-breaking fifteen-night sold-out concert series in 1999. The original leasing agreement is still in force, which benefits both the State of New Jersey and the artist. Springsteen's working-class New Jersey roots permeate his music, and it's what the Meadowlands audiences want to hear. As he emerged as a voice of the people, Springsteen was invited in July 1988 to perform in what was then East Germany, still sealed off by the Berlin Wall. An unbelievable 300,000 mostly young people attended his concert, which some reporters and political observers credit as the beginning of organized opposition to the regime and the fall of the wall the following year. In October 2009, Bruce Springsteen and the E Street Band's Wrecking

Left: Bruce "Boss" Springsteen is seen during one of the many concerts he and the E Street Band performed at the Byrne/Continental/Izod Arena and later in Giants Stadium. *New Jersey Sports and Exhibition Authority.*

Below: The Brenden Byrne Arena glowing at night during its initial season in 1981. *New Jersey Sports and Exhibition Authority.*

Ball Tour closed down the old Giants Stadium in the Meadowlands, the last event to appear at the eighty-thousand-seat football field that had hosted the New York Giants since 1976 and the New York Jets since 1984.

The band holding the record of the most single performances in the Meadowlands is the Grateful Dead, who appeared sixteen times in the 1980s. Queen appeared twice, with a separation of twenty-five years. Simon and Garfunkel, together again in October 2003, offered two concerts with the Everly Brothers, and Cher's two Farewell Tours took place in the Meadowlands in 2002 and 2005. The magical Elton John appeared at the Izod, as has Eric Clapton, the Who and AC/DC. Madonna, Billy Joel and U2, along with Janet Jackson, have filled the arena, and in 2014, the unpredictable Miley Cyrus produced a sold-out performance attended primarily by adolescent girls.

On March 14, 1986, Frank Sinatra, New Jersey's own "Old Blue Eyes" and the "Chairman of the Board," gave a virtuoso Meadowlands performance of his greatest classics that included "My Way," "Nancy," "My Kind of Town," "Without a Song," "For Once in My Life," "Nice and Easy," "Mack the Knife," "Moonlight in Vermont" and ten other timeless songs concluding with "New York, New York." The Chairman was seventy-one years old, and according to reviewers, he had gotten even better. Four years later, he returned to the Meadowlands for his seventy-fifth birthday concert and opened with "You Make Me Feel So Young." Longtime friends Liza Minnelli, Eydie Gorme and Steve Lawrence appeared on stage with him, and Liza and Frank sang "New York, New York," which engendered the greatest applause of the evening until Steve Lawrence led the twenty thousand concertgoers, on their feet, in a rendition of "Happy

Old Blue Eyes, Frank Sinatra, in an informal photograph taken at his home in Hoboken, circa 1946. *Courtesy of the Tom Austin family archive.*

Birthday Frank." In 2009, the Frank Sinatra album *Live in the Meadowlands*, which was recorded in 1986, was released.

Bon Jovi, the internationally acclaimed rock and heavy metal band, is one of the world's most influential musical artists. Jon Bon Jovi Jr., the band's frontman is a distinguished son of New Jersey, originally from Perth Amboy. Bon Jovi appeared in the Meadowlands at both the Izod Center and Giants Stadium. The only other band to accomplish that feat is Bruce Springsteen and the E Street Band. In October 1988, Bon Jovi embarked on the New Jersey Syndicate Tour, which ended in December 1991 after 232 performances throughout the world.

Top: Sinatra's "Live at the Meadowlands" album was released twenty-three years after his landmark performance at the Byrne Arena. *Courtesy of Tom Austin family archive.*

Left: Jon Bon Jovi Jr.—the internationally acclaimed songwriter, musician and political activist—has regularly appeared at the Meadowlands. John Bon Jovi Jr. is the frontman for the rock band Bon Jovi, one of the most listened-to bands in the world. *New Jersey Sports and Exhibition Authority.*

Jon Bon Jovi Jr. has moved from his early heavy mental image to a position of influence in national politics. Al Gore and President Obama have sought his council on environmental and family-strengthening issues. He supports extensive charitable endeavors and has had part ownerships of professional sport teams. While New Jersey fans love Bon Jovi, the band has returned the admiration by releasing their *New Jersey* album in 1988, which soared to the top of all music charts in the English-speaking world. And in 1989, *New Jersey* became the first American band album released in the Soviet Union. Bon Jovi's appearances in the Meadowlands, first at the arena and lately at MetLife Stadium, are a tribute to their greatest fans: the people of New Jersey who love this band of Jersey boys.

Presently, music in the Meadowlands is threatened due to the uncertain future of the Izod Center. The thirty-four-year-old arena has not been refurbished, and the building, which was never appealing, looks dated and tired. Events and teams have moved from the Meadowlands to the new Prudential Center in downtown Newark. The Prudential is bright and airy and lends itself to exhibitions and clever marketing displays, and even though it's location in traffic-bound Newark is not ideal, it has become a popular destination. The Prudential was built during the term of Newark's mayor Corey Booker, presently United States senator Booker, so the issue of whether or not every possible event would be held at the center was never in question.

Less than nine miles east of the Izod is the iconic Madison Square Garden in Midtown Manhattan. There has been a Madison Square Garden in New York City since the first one opened in 1879 adjacent to Madison Square Park at Twenty-Sixth Street. Designed by America's premier architect Stanford White, the building sported Moorish minarets and Spanish flourishes. White, a notorious playboy, was murdered in the Garden's rooftop restaurant by his lover's husband. The second Madison Square Garden was designed by theater architect Thomas Lamb, and it was located on Eighth Avenue and Fiftieth Street. This Garden, now known as the "old" Garden, was not a concert venue nor was it adequate for the television age of sports casting.

In the early 1960s, the New York Knicks basketball team and the New York Rangers hockey team ownership saw the need for better playing space in Manhattan. Ed Koch, the then mayor of New York, permitted the demolition of the magnificent Pennsylvania Station in order to build a new Madison Square Garden on the station's former site, a square block between

Seventh and Eighth Avenues and Thirty-first and Thirty-third Streets. Koch also slipped in real estate tax abatement for the new Garden that never expires. The Garden now calls itself "the world's most famous arena" and competes directly with the Izod. New Jersey Transit trains, PATH trains, Long Island Rail Road trains and the New York Subway System all converge under the Garden, bringing audience members from everywhere in the metropolitan area.

Work will begin soon on the American Dream, an indoor theme park and shopping destination located on the former Xanadu site adjacent to the Izod Center. There was speculation that the Izod would become part of the American Dream. There was also speculation that Izod would be closed and demolished and its space used to expand parking for MetLife Stadium.

Speculation about the future of the Izod Center ended on January 15, 2015, when the board of the New Jersey Sports and Exposition Authority (NJSEA) voted 10-2 to close the arena in response to the Christie administration. The decision was a surprise to Bergen County public officials and residents who conceded that the arena was troubled financially but served an important purpose in the life of the Meadowlands region. Events scheduled at the arena will be shifted to the Newark Prudential Center, the newer facility that enjoys support from state officials. The scores of schools and colleges that have held their graduation ceremonies in the Izod Center have had to find new venues, which has already proved to be an almost impossible task.

One fact is clear: the Izod Center will remain closed for two years. One hopeful plan reduces the arena's capacity to ten thousand comfortable seats, all with excellent views of the floor. This kind of building could attract audiences for long-term performances of theatrical shows of the *Lion King* or Cirque du Soleil genre. The American Dream theme park and retail center might incorporate the arena into its planned extravaganza of rides and attractions. There are several possibilities as to how to revitalize the thirty-four-year-old arena. Hopefully, one will be found, and the place that hosted so many great performers and great events will be saved from demolition.

CONCERTS IN THE MEADOWLANDS, BY JEFFREY KILEY

As a lifelong resident of Bergen County, I grew up in the heart of the Meadowlands in Rutherford in the 1960s, '70s and '80s and later moved to Ramsey in northern Bergen County, where I raised my family. As a young boy living in Rutherford, I would often ride my bicycle to the Meadowlands. In those early days, the Meadowlands had a drive-in movie theater and a fun place called Sportland that existed prior to the construction of the Meadowlands complex. I witnessed the construction of Giants Stadium, the racetrack, Brendan Byrne Arena in the '70s and recently the new MetLife Stadium. I also commuted to Wall Street on the New Jersey Transit Bergen Line trains through the meadows for over twenty-five years, witnessing the transformation of that vast area, including the building of the Secaucus transfer station.

One of my life's passions is music, and I have attended over one hundred rock concerts at all three venues over the last four decades. The list of performers includes such names as the Rolling Stones, the Grateful Dead, Eric Clapton, the Police, the Eagles and Van Halen, just to name a few. In total, there were over thirty different artists over forty years. Most notable is that I attended the initial concert at all three concert venues in the Meadowlands. In 1978, the first concert at Giants Stadium featured the Beach Boys, the Steve Miller Band and Pablo Cruise. In 1981, Bruce Springsteen was the first act to play at the Brendan Byrne Arena. I attended all six shows during that opening stand. Back in those days, you had to mail in money orders with return envelopes in hopes of getting tickets through a lottery system. Finally, I attended the first show at the new MetLife Stadium with Bon Jovi and the last show Bruce Springsteen and the E Street Band

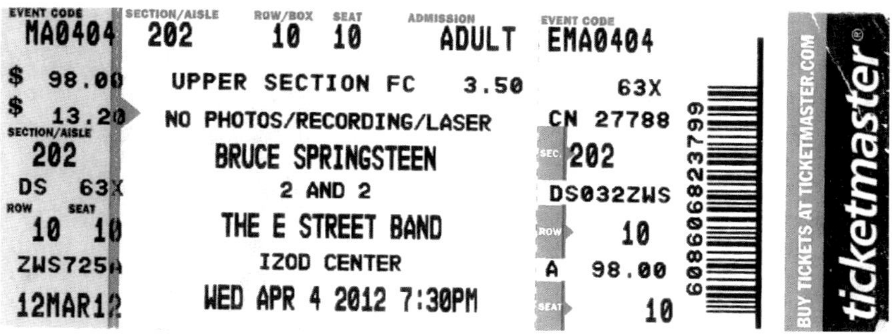

A ticket for the April 4, 2012 concert of Bruce Springsteen and the E Street Band at the Izod Center where they premiered "The Ties That Bind," "Johnny 99" and "Racing in the Street." *Courtesy of the Kopczynski family collection.*

performed at Giants Stadium during the Wrecking Ball Tour. Bruce actually wrote a song called "Wrecking Ball" as a tribute to the old Giants Stadium and its demolition. I have seen New Jersey's own Bruce Springsteen twenty-one times at both the arena and Giants Stadium. Bruce even joked during a show at the Izod Center. He said, "When we first played at this arena, it was named after a human being, then an airline, and it's now named after a sweater."

Jeffrey Kiley is the ultimate fan of music in the Meadowlands and a financial services executive.

7
THE SPORTS COMPLEX AND THE NEW JERSEY SPORTS AND EXPOSITION AUTHORITY

When the Meadowlands is mentioned on radio or television, everyone thinks of MetLife Stadium or Izod Arena, but almost no one even considers the Meadowlands region and its thirty square miles of development, environment and importance to New Jersey. You would think the development of the sports complex would have gone to the agency that was responsible for the planning and economic growth of the area. Instead, in 1970, William T. Cahill, the successor to Richard Hughes, moved forward with the concept of a sports complex in the Meadowlands that would include a stadium and racetrack. The idea, which was floated by the *Newark Star Ledger* in 1967, was to attract the New York Football Giants to a new stadium in the Meadowlands. The attraction for the Giants was a football-only stadium as opposed to playing in Yankee Stadium. Governor Cahill selected his treasurer, Joseph McCrane, to lead the effort to get the Giants to come to New Jersey.

There are two schools of thought as to why Cahill did not designate the Meadowlands Commission to lead the planning and construction of a new stadium and racetrack. One thought was the commission was still under legal challenges regarding the constitutionality of the act that created it. Some say Cahill was worried that the commission was just too much of an independent authority and could not be trusted to carry out the directives of the governor. The governor wanted his people in key positions on the board, which would include the treasurer and attorney general. Others have suggested the creation of the NJSEA and the construction of a sports venue would only enhance the image of the Meadowlands and, thus, increase values and spur growth around the complex. Cahill declared the Meadowlands to be the most valuable piece of property in the world. It was declared the site would lure residential and commercial construction and that at the end of the day, it would be the equivalent of a small city.

The commissioners of the HMDC fought long and hard with the governor and his advisors for the opportunity to be the lead agency but to no avail. During the period between the introduction of the Meadowlands Master Plan and its final adoption, the sport complex site was designated for the special uses area, which allowed for uses of regional importance, such as "sports stadiums, major education and health institutions, cultural facilities and other large scale development of that nature."

Placing the Sports Complex

On June 15, 1970, the commission contracted with the firm of Ewing, Cole, Erdman & Eubank to prepare a feasibility analysis of the various sites within the district for the construction of a sports complex. The consultants were charged to find a site where football, baseball, ice hockey, public recreation and hotel facilities were most suitable. That would have to take into consideration traffic, public transportation, sanitary and sewage treatment, soil conditions, depth to bedrock and utilities.

The commission supplied six sites to the consultant. Each of the six sites was evaluated and a recommendation made as to the suitability or unsuitability. The six original sites were as follows: Carlstadt, bordered by the western spur of the New Jersey Turnpike on the east, the Township of South Hackensack on the north, Moonachie Road on the west and Paterson Plank Road on the south (what is now the Kane Tract over six hundred acres of wetlands, which later became a battleground between environmentalist and developers); Secaucus and North Bergen, bounded on the west by the eastern spur of the New Jersey Turnpike (known today as the Guarini Tract, site of a one-hundred-acre plot of freshwater wetlands); Jersey City by Route 1 and 9 (areas adjacent to Tonelle Avenue); Secaucus, bordered by the Hackensack River on the west (the area next to Laurel Hill); Kearny, bounded south and west by the Harrison Kingsland Line and on the east by the western spur of the New Jersey Turnpike (the area now known as the Kearny Freshwater Marsh); East Rutherford, bordered by Paterson Plank Road on the north, Route 3 on the south, Berry's Creek on the west and Route 20 on the east (the site of the present complex). During the review, the criteria were that the site should be six hundred acres, the ingress and egress would be by car and public transportation had to be easy, bedrock should be seventy feet down for building support and it should be as rectangular as possible. The East Rutherford site was deemed the most suitable. Even with all this work, the commission was not successful in convincing Trenton it should build the complex. The commission did get some concessions in the legislation that gave it a seat at the NJSEA, and the issue of how the commission would be funded in the future was addressed by language that would provide the HMDC 40 percent of the net profits of the sports complex for its operating budget.

Capturing the Giants

The governor assigned Joseph McCrane, the state treasurer, to lead the state's efforts in getting the Giants to come to New Jersey. McCrane increased acreage of the sports complex to 750 to accommodate a racetrack. There were no racetracks that generated enough revenue to pay the principal and interest of the bonds for the entire complex. The approach made sure the state would not have to bear the burden of paying off the bonds. McCrane was no stranger to the racing industry, having served as general manager of the Garden State Race Track, which was owned by his father-in-law, Eugene Mori. On May 10, 1971, Governor Cahill signed into law the New Jersey Sports and Exposition Authority Act. Three months later, the State of New Jersey and the Giants had a deal. Governor Cahill and Giants owner Wellington Mara unveiled the designs for the new stadium. The plan faced its first obstacle when an angry New York governor, Nelson Rockefeller, called for a rival sports complex in Queens, which caused investors to become squeamish about the New Jersey bonds for the new complex. Only when the state puts its moral obligation behind the bonds did New Jersey companies and banks step in and underwrite the financing. By that time, the cost of the complex had grown to $302 million and eventually topped out at $342 million.

The 750-acre site in East Rutherford was the site of old landfills with a combination of wetlands, industrial-use structures, oil companies and a catering facility. The landfill was an active operation that took only Brooklyn garbage. The chief engineer of the commission, George Cascino, and members of his staff confronted the nighttime dumping operation and went to court to put an end to the illegal landfilling. He recalled that it was a scary confrontation with the operators of the illegal dump, who weren't used to having their activities questioned.

Although construction on the Meadowlands complex began in 1972, McCrane—who had been the finance chairman of Governor Cahill's campaign—resigned that year amid allegations of campaign fraud in the Cahill administration, and he could not see the project through. Some of the charges stemmed from an engineering firm working on the sports complex project.

Senator Ray Bateman, who later became the chairman of the Sports and Exposition Authority, recalls the groundbreaking in this way, "It was in the middle of this freaking, steamy, smelly, miserable swamp," he said. "That's what it was, with a big fence around it with a platform from which we were all making speeches to ourselves, and around us there were [*sic*] a circle of environmentalists who were screaming and yelling how bad this project was going to be to this beautiful area."

There were several lawsuits filed as a result of the passage of the sports authority law. The Audubon Society filed suit based on the environmental challenged that the project violated the Public Trust Doctrine because the wetlands on the site were once flowed by the tide, and the Audubon argued that the act permitted the granting, leasing or conveying of riparian lands without compensation. East Rutherford and South Hackensack filed suit based on whether the stadium and racetrack could be considered a public purpose. Monmouth Park Jockey Club (represented by Robert Wilnetz, who became a New Jersey Supreme Court chief justice) claimed that there was no constitutional basis for state ownership of a racetrack. The authority filed a suit to consolidate all the lawsuits against it to save time so it could start the project and meet the timetable to construct the stadium.

The perennial winner of the Meadowlands Indy-Pole car race, Mario Andretti, holds his first-place trophy aloft after winning the high stakes event on June 28, 1987. The 1.68-mile track actually snaked through the Giants Stadium parking lots and around the Byrne Arena. Andretti drove a Lola T 8700. The car was owned by actor Paul Newman. *New Jersey Sports and Exhibition Authority.*

In 1971, the court issued its opinion, finding the NJSEA law viable and that the project could move forward. The state supreme court concurred with the superior court's opinion in May 1972. On the environmental issue, Judge Pashman wrote:

> *I am satisfied that the Legislature has given much consideration to the environmental and ecological issues. In any case, the issue is not relevant at this time. The day may come when a decision or act by the Authority will affect the environment. At that time judicial and/or administrative relief, if necessary, will undoubtedly be available. For example, if after consultation with the Authority, the Department of Environmental Protection claims the project will have ill effects, it has the machinery necessary to pursue the matter further. The court must presume that the Department will serve vigorously. And when building is undertaken one day, all legal requirements outlined in anti-pollution legislation, in upgrading waste treatment facilities and in maintaining an ecological balance will be enforced. I cannot agree with public counsel*

> *that the State will stand committed in the absence of an immediate environmental hearing. I fully agree that the public should be and is entitled to a further opportunity to be heard on the environmental and ecological overtones of the legislation. Although the court may not have the facilities or power to be able to police the ecological factors, it may perhaps oversee the actions of the administrative agencies in this vital area. It is before these agencies that experts may appear if the Authority is violating any provision of environmental law. But to determine that this is not the juncture for such a hearing is not to deny the right. Every piece of legislation carries its advantages and disadvantages. The mere passage of the act is not enough to bring about judicial intervention. And this is as it should be, because in the final analysis government by judges is inferior to government by legislators.*

On June 9, 1972, the New Jersey Department of Environmental Protection and the Hackensack Meadowlands Development Commission issued a public notice that indicated that a joint hearing on the sports complex's environmental impacts would be empaneled. The authority was directed to prepare an environmental impact statement (EIS), and all parties that participated in the lawsuits were invited to prepare materials and were told they could call witnesses. Site, suitability and every element of environmental impacts were reviewed by the hearing officers. For each element of the EIS, recommendations were provided. The process moving forward was known as the hearing officers' report. For every development on the complex, the process would be the same.

The hearing officers suggested that the 132-acre Berry's Creek Tidal Marsh be purchased and restored even though it was known to have significant concentration of heavy metals, in particular mercury. Using a suggested scraping method, they recommended that the marsh be brought back to its pre-1900 vegetation. If that method of remediation was not viable, other methods should be explored. The NJDEP and the HMDC also recommended the construction, financing and maintenance of an environmental education center.

Environmental Education

Ultimately, the mercury contamination of the Berry's Creek Tidal Marsh prevented any action on the site, including the construction of an environment center. The HMDC approached the sports authority with the proposal that the two should enter into an agreement to locate and build the environment center. When the commission decided to build its complex in Lyndhurst, the environment center became part of the complex. The sports authority provided its share of the costs to build the center, but Green Acres and the HMDC added to the project a visitor's center over the Kingsland Marsh and Impoundment. The complex was built at the foot of the Bergen County landfill and the Kingsland Marsh. The marsh was designated as a landfill prior to the commission's creation. It was a symbolic gesture of the end of the indiscriminate dumping of garbage.

The hearing officers' report stated that the sports authority should be responsible for a fund to "operate and maintain" the environment center. The finance and support of the environment center from the sports complex ended in the mid-1990s with the Whitman administration deciding the commission should foot the entire bill and that the sports complex should worry only about the sports complex. The entire 1972 hearing officers' report was made a condition of the approval of the Army Corps of Engineers permit to fill the wetlands. That language still stands in the federal permit but the Whitman administration required the Meadowlands Commission to pass a resolution indicating the condition was no longer in effect. That resolution did not or could not negate the permit. The sports authority later committed $600,000 for the expansion of the Science and Education Building at the commission site when the Mills Project was being considered. Unfortunately, today we find the commission saying it can no longer fund the center at the level it once did. Ramapo College of New Jersey, which has had a contract to operate the center for over fourteen years, will now be operating it on a limited basis. (Over twenty thousand schoolchildren used to attend programs annually.)

The report made forty-six recommendations. It ranged from the capacity of the Bergen County's Little Ferry Sewer Treatment Plant to handle the sanitary sewage from the complex (which today is still an issue) to energy use and how to handle the horse manure generated by the racetrack. The report directed the manure to be sent to a composting operation for mushroom farming. One of the more interesting recommendations from the hearing officers was the issue of traffic congestion and the call for the sports complex to develop a comprehensive mass transit system of buses and trains. It was suggested that the Erie Lackawanna passenger line be the focal point for train service. It was only in 2005 that the plan for a train station and a rail spur moved forward with significant support from the Port Authority of New York and New Jersey.

A Day at the Races

On September 1, 1976, the Meadowlands Racetrack became the first part of the complex to open its doors. More than 42,000 people attended the first night of harness racing. Governor Brendan Byrne attended the opening and rode in an open carriage on the track. The governor, who has a great sense of humor, had just come off the battle for the state's first income tax and recalled riding in the horse-drawn carriage waving to the crowd, but he noted there were not many in the crowd who waved back with all their fingers. Giants Stadium opened on October 10, 1976, as 76,042 fans watched the New York Giants lose to the Dallas Cowboys, 24–14.

The racetrack became the premier track in North America for harness racing, getting the top horses with the largest purses in the sport with crowds on weekends of twenty-five to thirty thousand patrons. The track was the cash machine that McCrane envisioned not only for the sports complex but also for the state of New Jersey. The complex went far and wide to get pari-mutuel employees for the track. There was a bus every night that would pick up employees from locations near Monmouth Park and Garden State Park in Cherry Hill and bring them to the Big M. Many seasoned veterans of pari-mutuels were characters in their own right. The veteran pari-mutuel operators were mixed in with local residents who received the jobs through local political figures. They were the fortunate ones who worked at good salaries six days a week and, sometimes, for almost three hundred days a year. Each year, the tracks would apply to the racing commission for racing days for their track. Meadowlands would always get the most days. These employees worked with no sick days or vacation, and if you made a mistake at the window, the mistake would come out of your pocket. Pay was good, and you received good benefits. Unfortunately for some, the betting temptation became too great, and some employees were removed either by management or the state police. Their gambling addiction became too great, especially when they started to use the track's money for betting.

On August 4, 1984, trotter Historic Freight won the Hambletonian, harness racing's Kentucky Derby, at the Meadowlands Racetrack. A $1,219,000 purse was divided among the win, place and show finishers. *New Jersey Sports and Exhibition Authority.*

1925-1955 Polo Grounds… 1956-1973 Yankee Stadium…

1976 GIANTS STADIUM

Today, October 10, 1976 marks the opening of Giants Stadium. This date will take its place next to the two other Sundays in October which have marked the beginnings of new eras in the team's history.

On October 18, 1925 the late Tim Mara, founder of the National Football League in New York, led his team into the Polo Grounds against the Frankford Yellow Jackets and the Giants went on to play at the old ball park for the next thirty years. During those years the Giants won three World Championships, 1927, 1934, 1938, and were eight times Eastern Champions.

October 21, 1956 the Giants opened their first season at Yankee Stadium against the Pittsburgh Steelers. They went on to win the World Championship that year and before the final gun closed the "Stadium Era", on September 23, 1973, the Giants had earned six more Eastern Championships.

Entering Giants Stadium in their 52nd season, the Giants have played for the World Championship fourteen times, a record unequalled by any other team in the NFL.

To comemmorate the opening of Giants Stadium, the Giants have prepared this souvenir gift-pack for all the fans attending today's game with the Dallas Cowboys. In addition to the Stadium picture, the pack contains an opening day bumper sticker and an exact reproduction of the original game program from the first home game ever played by the Giants.

The stadium picture was part of the souvenir gift pack given to fans attending the opening of Giants Stadium on October 10, 1976. *Courtesy of the Kopczynski family collection.*

The "Giants Stadium I Was There Opening Day" bumper sticker was given out to fans on October 10, 1976, the opening day game against the Dallas Cowboys, which the Giants lost. The sticker is a winner if you own one, however, because few have survived. *Courtesy of the Kopczynski family collection.*

The track also had its effects on other harness racing tracks like Yonkers Raceway in New York, which closed for a while and came back eventually as a racino, and Freehold Raceway in New Jersey.

It was also a great day for the Meadowlands Commission financially. As part of the incentive agreed on under Cahill that kept the commission out of the development of the sports complex, the agency was to get 40 percent of the net profits of the complex. In the late 1970s to early '80s, the number was approaching $10 million per year. The definition of "net" profit came into play about the same time the commission was to get its funding. The commission's budget from 1970 to '80 was a loan from the state treasury. The Meadowlands Commission was never given a direct state appropriation. The enabling legislation was structured so that the commission was to receive its revenue from the reclamation and development of land in the Meadowlands and solid waste. When the commission saw the transition from Hughes to Cahill, the approach became very different. Through new Cahill appointments and continued political pressure from the towns, the independence of the commission diminished, which limited its powers.

With its first payment from the sports authority, the commission paid the treasury for the loans for its operation. The commission received one check the following year, and that was the last check received under the statutory language. It was decided that the commission had to strike out on its own financially. The treasurer decided that the HMDC should come up with a series of recommendations on how it was going to fund itself. With not one of the proposals acceptable to the HMDC commissioners and the treasurer, state appropriation started for a ten-year period. The agency eventually became financially self-sufficient through its solid waste operations.

With the success of the complex, in 1977, plans started for new arena to be built on the site. Several locations were examined on the site, including areas adjacent to the stadium. That plan would have eliminated close to two thousand parking spaces. That would not have worked out, considering the Giants' lease required twenty-four thousand spaces to be available for game day at all times. The site chosen was the site that was initially designed in the 1972 hearing officers' report as an area for future hotel development or possible arena. The site was separated by Route 20, known today as Route 120. That brought up a logistics issue: where would people park at events in the stadium and arena and how would they cross busy Route 120? A pedestrian bridge and a new system of service roads connected the sites. The issues of more traffic came up again but were never really addressed.

Pelé played for the New York Cosmos from 1975 to 1977 in the Meadowlands. He was designated "World Player of the Century" by the soccer world and "Athlete of the Century" by the International Olympic Committee in 1999. *New Jersey Sports and Exhibition Authority.*

A capacity crowd watches the World Cup in Giants Stadium in 1994. *New Jersey Sports and Exhibition Authority.*

THE BYRNE/CONTINENTAL/IZOD ARENA

The arena opened July 2, 1981, with the first of six sold-out shows by Bruce Springsteen. The board of commissioners at the sports authority decided it was going to name the arena for Governor Byrne and the new aquarium in Camden after Governor Tom Kean. The names lasted for a while until the issues of naming rights became part of negotiations with the Nets and the Devils. The Brendan Byrne Arena became the Continental Airline Arena when the airline put up $29 million. When the naming rights deal was announced, NJSEA chairman Michael Francis said at a news conference, "If a Republican's name had been on it, it still would have come down. There's nothing personal. This was based solely on economics." That was not very convincing to Mrs. Byrne, who has held a grudge against Governor Whitman for the name change. The Continental deal paid $750,000 in 1996, $1.5 million in 1997, $2.25 million in 1998 and $1.5 million a year from 1999 to 2007. It also provided the sports authority $700,000 worth of airline tickets. The tickets could be liquidated and sold to brokers, or they could be sold to the teams that played at the arena. The sports authority officials did their best to sell the tickets. To this day, the authority still has some tickets left over that United Airline has agreed to honor. Following the Devils' leaving in 2007, Continental Airlines opted out of the naming rights agreement, and the NJSEA signed an agreement with Izod for five years. The company's deal paid $1.4 million per year for the first two years of the agreement, and when the Nets left, it dropped to $750,000. The arena also hosted tennis championships and Olympic qualifying events on a regular basis.

The other little-known fact that had financial ramifications on the economics of running the arena was the requirement that the NJSEA hold dates open for both the Devils and the Nets, prohibiting the agency booking concerts and other family shows, which were money makers for the complex. The dates put on hold went from the beginning of the team's preseason through the playoffs and the championship series. The dates were not released until it was official that the teams would not make it to the playoffs or the championship. This requirement could block out more than one-third of the available dates at the arena. The arena was losing $4.5 million a year just for the privilege of having the teams at the arena. The irony was that the arena could have been profitable without the teams. The arena still made a net profit from its concerts and other popular events that attracted sellout crowds.

Above: Tennis champion Chris Evert with Governor Brenden Byrne prior to her winning the grueling round-robin match against Tracy Austin in the season-ending event held at the Byrne Arena in December 1981. Evert, who had won Wimbledon that year, lost to Austin in the semifinals of the tournament. *New Jersey Sports and Exhibition Authority.*

Left: Tracy Austin, after winning the Toyota Tennis Championship in the Byrne Arena in December 1981. Austin beat Martina Navratilova in the three-set final match. *Photo by Gayle Burns.*

Tennis great Ivan Lendl in the final match of the Meadowlands Tennis Challenge on October 9, 1985. Lendl defeated John McEnroe to win the invitational tournament. *New Jersey Sports and Exhibition Authority.*

Changing the name on the arena and selling the naming rights started with the difficult negotiations in 1995 with the New Jersey Devils, which insisted on concessions to help them to get out of financial difficulties. Governor Byrne was part of a group who sought an NHL franchise for the Meadowlands Arena. When New Jersey developer Arthur Imperatore—president of A-P-A Transport Corporation, the nation's fourth-largest interstate freight trucking company—purchased the Colorado Rockies in 1978, everyone thought it would be an automatic transfer to the state. Imperatore was not allowed to move the franchise by the NHL, however, because there were no temporary facilities that were suitable until the arena was finished. Imperatore sold the team to Houston Astros owner Dr. John McMullen in 1982. With the arena now

Billy Olson about to set a new world record for the high jump in the 1986 Olympic Invitational held in the Byrne Arena. Olson, from Abilene, Texas, competed in the 1988 summer Olympics. *New Jersey Sports and Exhibition Authority.*

completed, McMullen, a native of Montclair, announced that he would move the team to New Jersey, where they became known as the New Jersey Devils.

In 1991, the NJSEA's responsibilities were broadened radically, when the legislature approved a $418 million financing package that included money to refinance sports complex debt, build a new convention center in Atlantic City and expand athletic facilities at Rutgers University. The legislation committed tax dollars to pay for debt for the first time ever. It was the beginning of a long and winding road downward for

Right: Patrick Ewing accepting a contribution to the Georgetown University student scholarship fund after the Hoyas defeated Seton Hall 90–70 in the Byrne Arena on January 8, 1985. *New Jersey Sports and Exhibition Authority.*

Below: The U.S. Olympic Invitational Women's sixty-meter sprint in the Byrne Arena was held in 1986. *Left to right*: #7 Alice Jackson, #1 Evelyn Ashford, #5 Marlene Ohey-Page and #16 Pam Marshall. *New Jersey Sports and Exhibition Authority.*

the sports authority's financial picture. The legislature decided it was going to expand the role of the authority and, at the same time, increase its debt load while bringing state tax dollars into the equation. The then candidate for New Jersey governor Christine Todd Whitman, at a press conference at the sports complex, stated, "It's time to consider auctioning off the Meadowlands Sports Complex." Whitman blasted the New Jersey Sports and Exposition Authority for rewarding a dozen top-level executives with merit raises at a time when operating income had declined and tax dollars were being used to help repay sports complex debt. "There seems to be a direct correlation," Whitman said. "The worse you do, the more you get paid." Whitman called for a study into the feasibility of turning the publicly owned sports complex over to private ownership or management and for an audit of the authority's operations. "There are several different ways of doing it," Whitman said. "You could lease out, you could have a public-private partnership, or you could move toward total privatization. The whole range needs to be looked at. I am a great supporter of sports," Whitman said. "Each one of these facilities is a great addition to the state, but the real question

The 1999 Women's World Cup began play in the Meadowlands stadium on June 19. It was a milestone in the development of women's sports and was won by the American team. The team photo features Governor Whitman with coach Tony DiCicco to her left, Donna de Varona to her right, team captain Carla Overbeck behind microphone, Julie Foudy in front and Brandy Chastain to her right. *New Jersey Sports and Exhibition Authority.*

is should the taxpayers be paying the burden for these—especially when you see a clear downward trend in revenues." The legislation committed tax dollars to repaying sports authority debt for the first time ever, but the package never went before voters in a referendum. "It's not against the language of the constitution, but it's certainly against the spirit of the constitution of this state," Whitman said. "That's a trend that bothers me exceedingly and something that should be stopped." However, during her term, the governor borrowed $3.4 billion to make long-term pension payments and created a large debt obligation without referendum.

A Devil of a Deal

McMullen started his quest for lease concessions from his landlord, the NJSEA, in 1995. Governor Whitman was a famous Devils fan and could be often found in McMullen's box. The squabble over the Devils lease started in earnest after the win of the Stanley Cup that year over the Detroit Red Wings. Dr. McMullen was looking for more money and more control over the arena. He was willing to listen to offers from Nashville. Nashville offered the Devils a $20 million relocation fee, cheap rent and a guarantee to keep 100.0 percent of ticket and advertising sales and 97.5 percent of the luxury box revenues.

The NJSEA went to court to stop the Devils from breaking its lease. In NJSEA court papers, president and CEO Bob Mulcahy pointed to eleven different concessions over time totaling $33 million made by the state to the Devils. They included three different amendments to the leases, deferment of loans and rental payments for building offices for the team and the purchasing tickets. Whitman, a huge Devils fan, was not one to believe in giving up the store, especially for sports teams, but NJSEA Chairman Peter Levine made the underlying feeling of the state very clear, "The Devils bring national prestige to New Jersey. If they leave, what would it do to the image of the Meadowlands, how many more New Jersey jokes would there be, how many jobs would be lost?" The governor brought her husband, John Whitman, into the negotiations and in some instances without the NJSEA top officials. The deal was struck with the Devils. The new deal called for the authority to forgive a $1.65 million loan to the team; guarantee $3.2 million in additional revenue from new advertising in the first five years of the lease, with an increase to $5.2 million at the end of the fifth year of the lease and an additional $2 million coming from new seating and enhancements; provide the team with a larger portion of the profits from concession, parking and the arena restaurant; cut the rent in the last six years of the lease to 8 percent of the gross ticket receipts from home games; purchase up to one thousand season tickets; and make improvements to the arena, including additional luxury boxes and club seating. In return, the Devils signed a new twelve-year lease. The concessions and investment cost the sports complex a large financial commitment. It took only two years before McMullen was threatening to leave the Continental Arena. He unveiled a new plan to build a new arena over the Hoboken train station. He envisioned a twenty-thousand-seat arena with 150 luxury boxes that would be privately owned. Without the cooperation of the state, McMullen backed off the idea. Devils owner John McMullen agreed to sell his hockey team to the YankeeNets for $175 million.

The Nets and the "Seven"

The New Jersey Nets moved into the arena in 1981 when they were purchased by a group of seven local businessmen, who became known as the "Secaucus Seven," led by Alan N. Cohen and Joseph Taub. After a lengthy ownership of the franchise and numerous attempts to improve the financial situation of the team, the Secaucus Seven finally sold the team in 1998 to a group of local real estate developers led by Raymond Chambers and Lewis Katz, who wanted to move the team to Newark. Eventually, Chambers and Katz became part of the YankeeNets holding company that, along with the Devils, hoped to facilitate the move.

Like with the Devils, the sports authority was powerless with the Nets when they wanted to renegotiate their lease. The lease with the Nets gave the team an extension on repaying a $1.8 million debt in exchange for the right of first refusal if the team were put up for sale. That way, if someone wanted to buy the Nets and move the pro basketball team to another state, the sports authority could step in and buy the team and then resell it to local investors or retain control itself.

The authority forgave the Nets the outstanding debt, gave the team concession revenue of approximately $10 million over five years, a greater percentage of parking revenue and 30 percent of the

Sam Bowie, Nets center, played from 1989 to 1993 in the Byrne Arena. *New Jersey Sports and Exhibition Authority.*

naming rights deal. All those concessions came at the expense of the authority. The debt service payment burden continued to grow. At the time of the lease agreement, payments on bonds were $37.5 million. With less revenue coming in, the state had to pay $17 million to help pay off the bonds.

8

WHO'S PLAYING AT THE STADIUM?

Governor Whitman was appointed U.S. Environmental Protection Agency administrator and, on her last day in office, announced a tentative agreement with the YankeeNets the owners the Devils and Nets. The agreement called for the state to provide a portion of the funding for the $325 million arena that would be built in Newark. The YankeeNets characterized the announcement not as an agreement at all but an outline of basic terms as a starting point of negotiations. Under the New Jersey Constitution, the state senate president Donald DiFrancesco was next in line in succession to the governor. On becoming acting governor and still staying on as senate president, DiFrancesco made it very clear that he did not agree with the Whitman plan. Without DiFrancesco's approval, the plan would not move forward because it needed legislative approval. While he agreed the state should make attempts to keep the teams in New Jersey, he indicated the need to determine the future of the complex in East Rutherford while the Newark arena was being discussed.

Governor DiFrancesco, a longtime veteran of the statehouse, saw this opportunity as an avenue of not only leaving his legacy of building an arena in Newark but also of finding a way to revitalize the sports complex, which was approaching twenty-five years, a required balancing act if he was going to run for governor. He was looking at a strategy that combined an urban revitalization project in Newark while stabilizing the sports complex in Bergen County and its 100,000 Republican votes. The racetrack, the cash machine of the complex, was seeing revenues

Lower-tier spectators at Giants Stadium in 1977 enjoying a field-level view of a Cosmos soccer game. *New Jersey Sports and Exhibition Authority.*

continue to downslide because of the growth of gambling in Atlantic City and the generational gap of those who enjoyed horse racing. Coupled with those facts was the undeniable reality that the sports complex debt was choking the agency.

Governor DiFrancesco brought in investment banker Lewis Eisenberg to develop a plan for an arena in Newark and the Meadowlands Sports Complex in East Rutherford. Eisenberg was the chairman of the Port Authority of New York and New Jersey. Eisenberg was also one of the DiFrancesco campaign's major fundraisers. Eisenberg faced a difficult assignment: get a deal with YankeeNets, make sure the state was not saddled with additional debt from sports facilities that became obsolete and solidify the sports complex as a job and economic center for the Meadowlands region. The requirement to satisfy South Jersey interests in the package became an issue for assembly Speaker Jack Collins, who vowed not to move any bill that did not include something for his area. He sought $20 million for an athletics facility at Rowan University, where Collins worked and studied; $20 million for a convention center in Pennsauken; $1 million for a rowing facility near Camden; and $3 million for two other entertainment districts in South Jersey. Added to the equation was the requirement by YankeeNets that Continental Arena be demolished.

The Eisenberg plan coupled with an arena in Newark was a ten-year plan that would create a "world-class, family-oriented, seven-day-a-week destination." The project would have been financed with incremental tax revenue, meaning taxes generated on site and through leases with developers. It was also proposed that the revenue from the complex would be used to pay the authority's significant debt. To address the issue of traffic congestions, $350 million was to be released from the Transportation Trust Fund to construct a mass transit hub for the site and to realign roads. The plan included a village center, a family entertainment and retail district, a realignment of Route 120—which at the time cut through the Meadowlands complex—a new football stadium for the New York Jets and Giants, thirty-one thousand new parking spaces and a four thousand-seat amphitheater.

Governor DiFrancesco ultimately decided not to run for governor, which sealed the fate of the Newark/Meadowlands plans. The future of the arena was left to Governor Jim McGreevey.

The wrangling on how to fund the arena came to an end with the City of Newark entering into a new lease deal with the Port Authority of New York and New Jersey for Newark Airport and the Port of Newark. The new lease allowed the port authority to rename Newark to Newark Liberty International Airport and increase the term of the leases from 2031 to 2065 in exchange for $265 million. Many questioned why the city would spend so much money on an arena when the municipality had so many other critical needs like housing and schools. Others argued the arena would be a springboard for the revitalization of the city.

No More Nets

After thirty-five seasons in New Jersey, the Nets returned to the state of New York in 2012 to play in the new Barclays Center in Brooklyn as the Brooklyn Nets. YankeeNets would ultimately fail in its attempts to secure a deal with Newark to construct a new arena in the city. By that point in time, tensions among the management of the Yankees, Nets and Devils had caused a rift, and a decision was made to split the group up. After a short bidding process, the group secured a deal with real estate developer Bruce Ratner to buy the team for $300 million, defeating a similar offer by Charles Kushner and Senator Jon S. Corzine of New Jersey. Ratner had purchased the team with the intent of moving it to a new arena in Brooklyn, which was to be a centerpiece of the large-scale Atlantic Yards development. Ratner never had an interest in being a team owner. The prize was the development at the Atlantic Yards.

The Devils were purchased and finally moved to Newark prior to the 2007–08 season. The team continued to have financial difficulties until it was bought by the owners of the Philadelphia 76ers.

As all the drama developed with the Nets and Devils, the other sports teams on the complex had their own ideas about what they were entitled to and where their future playing field might be. John Mara, then vice-president of the Giants, demanded $300 million in renovations to the stadium in 2003. He contended that the lease, which was extended in 1995 until 2026, gave the team the right to the renovations under the provisions that the state would provide it a state-of-the-art facility. The team proposed taking control of the operations of the stadium and keeping a majority of the profits from the stadium. The NJSEA president and CEO of the NJSEA at the time was George Zoffinger. Zoffinger was a highly successful businessman who was brought in by McGreevey to determine if he could either stop the financial bleeding at the sports authority and/or break it down for the purpose of selling its assets to the private sector. He was very outspoken about the Giants' request for upgrades and the determination of what a state-of-the-art stadium meant in the lease agreement. He was adamant that he was not going to be part of any plan that was going to cost the taxpayers any money and, at the same time, increase the debt of the NJSEA. The Giants made it clear that, as one of the premier franchises in the NFL, it was lagging behind in revenues compared to the other franchises. As were the claims of the Devils and Nets, the demand was about the ability to have club seating and many more luxury boxes. The "luxury box envy" came at a time when the NFL was seeing more and more stadiums being built. In response, Mara stated to John Brennan of the *Record*, the long-standing observer of everything at the Meadowlands complex, "We play in an outdated building with a tough lease," Mara said. "We're not attempting to cry poverty to anybody, but we are asking them to comply with those promises that they made in 1995." In 1995, the NJSEA reduced the Giants' lease by reducing the rent of 15 percent of gross ticket sales to 10 percent, and the definition of "state of the art" was added, which included the "quality of the field, the lighting, and the seating and other aspects under that description." Zoffinger believed the definition of "state of the art facility" meant, in fact, the arena needed some renovation but nowhere near what the Giants were thinking. As for the Jets, the team stated its intention was to go back to

Giants quarterback Phil Simms ready to fire a pass during the October 20, 1985 game against the Washington Redskins, won by the Giants 17–3. Simms played for the Giants during his entire fourteen year career (1979–93) and was voted MVP of Super Bowl XXI, in which the Giants defeated the Denver Broncos. *New Jersey Sports and Exhibition Authority.*

New York when the proposed West Side Stadium project was made public. It opted not even to be part of the conversation about Giants Stadium. The war clouds between the Giants and the NJSEA were stirring and looming large in New Jersey. All of this was happening despite no team using the complex, though the Devils acknowledged New Jersey as their home. With no one backing off, it was anticipated that a lawsuit was coming.

In the meantime, the City of New York negotiated with the Jets for their use of a stadium that was part of the effort to bring the Olympics to the New York City area. It was anticipated that the Olympics would also use New Jersey facilities, including Giants Stadium. The proposed Jets Stadium, which had an estimated cost of $1.4 billion, along with an expanded Jacob K. Javits Convention Center, required the Jets to contribute $800 million to the construction, with the City and State of New York coming up with the remaining $600 million. Mayor Giuliani proposed an increase in the sales tax to pay for the city's share of the costs. The stadium would have been located in the rectangle bounded by Eleventh and Twelfth Avenues and Thirtieth and Thirty-third Streets of Manhattan, and the design called

The New York Jets have played in the Meadowlands stadium, now MetLife stadium, since 1984, after leaving New York's Shea Stadium, where they had played for twenty years. *New Jersey Sports and Exhibition Authority.*

for a dome. The Giants never wanted a dome on their stadium because they felt the late fall early winter weather of the Northeast would give them a playing advantage. The New York stadium was going to be built on a deck over the West Side rail yards, which are a critical point of train access into Manhattan from New Jersey.

By September 2005, the New York Jets informed New York's Metropolitan Transportation Authority that it would not proceed with its plan for the stadium. The battle for the stadium was a bitterly fought entanglement among political figures, neighborhood groups and mayors. State assembly Speaker Sheldon Silver, a Democrat of Manhattan, blocked the project from going forward, citing competing concerns about redevelopment of the World Trade Center site and Lower Manhattan. In January 2015, Silver was indicted by a federal grand jury for fraud, extortion and conspiracy in connection with his position as the New York assembly Speaker.

The Jets opened discussion with the New Jersey Sports Authority and the Giants about a joint venture between the teams but also looked at the possibility of joining the Mets in the venture to build a stadium in Flushing. The New Jersey option was the one that prevailed. Zoffinger's position on the Giants and Jets proved to be true. He originally wanted to hold off negotiations with the Giants until July, by which time, he predicted the Jets stadium deal would have collapsed, leaving the team with little choice but to remain in the Meadowlands. Richard Codey became governor and continued as senate president after the resignation of Jim McGreevey. He didn't accept Zoffinger's reasoning. Governor Codey was an avid sports fan, and he felt the need to tie down the Giants immediately. He was not going to chance that they were going back to New York. He said the deal with the Giants was good for the taxpayers of the state. The Codey/Zoffinger feud escalated on a personal level and became public. Codey refused to allow Zoffinger to proceed with any further negotiations and made it clear he, as governor, was going to make the decision on the stadium deal with the Giants. Codey refused to wait for the Jets' decision. He grew more and more impatient with Zoffinger and continued to publicly complain about him. Codey said of Zoffinger, "He has essentially presided over the destruction of the sports authority. The purpose of the sports authority was to bring sports teams to New Jersey, and they're all leaving. We've lost too many teams." He went further by saying, "As a result of the Giants' coming over here, we built a whole new economy then an arena. As a result, Bergen County and that whole region in the state have grown tremendously. We're losing that?" Zoffinger felt the deal was a sweetheart deal for the Giants. "The details of this deal will come out," he said, "and the people will decide for themselves." The relationship got to an all-time low when Zoffinger referred to the governor as the cartoon character Spongebob Squarepants.

Codey said Zoffinger was wrong because he did not include the intangible benefits presented by the teams. He insisted the $124 million of debt that the state incurred on the old stadium was not really a subsidy. He made the point that the original $75 million of debt the stadium carried when it opened twenty-nine years earlier would already have been retired if the state hadn't refinanced the facility to pay for other projects. Among them were the New Jersey State Aquarium in Camden ($32 million), the Atlantic City Convention Center ($268 million), Historic Boardwalk Hall ($100 million), the Wildwood Convention Center ($68 million) and the Rutgers Stadium

Technicians installing new signage atop the New York Giants Training Center in the Meadowlands. *Courtesy of Christopher Schifano and Network Graphic Imaging, LLC.*

Installations of new graphics over the entrance to the New York Giants Training Center, which, for a decade, had sported the Timex logo. *Courtesy of Christopher Schifano and Network Graphic Imaging, LLC.*

Quarterback Jeff Hostetler, no. 15, played for the New York Giants for eight seasons and led them to victory in Super Bowl XXV over the Buffalo Bills. *New Jersey Sports and Exhibition Authority.*

expansion ($100 million). Carl Goldberg agreed the debt would have been gone had it not been for the added obligations.

In response to Codey's action, Mara said to the *Bergen Record*, "We welcome the governor assuming control of these negotiations. And hopefully that will help bring this to a conclusion." Mara accused Zoffinger of adding conditions at the last minute that held up the negotiation and forced the Giants into court to invoke the state-of-the-art facility clause.

Under the terms of the deal, the Giants would pay $6.3 million in rent and payment in lieu of taxes for seventy-five acres of the stadium, a practice facility on the western end of the complex and infrastructure improvements. Zoffinger complained that the rent was extremely low and that this land was very valuable on the open Bergen County market. The Giants would be allowed naming rights and have control over other activities on the sports complex site. He emphasized the fact that the state would no longer be generating enough revenue to retire the outstanding debt of the existing stadium once it was torn down. Carl Goldberg, chairman of the sports authority board, was caught in the middle of this war and ultimately had enough votes to approve the Giants' deal.

MetLife Stadium Appears

The NJSEA conducted a taxable sale of bonds that refunded portions of state contract bonds and sports complex debt that the authority sold from 1992 to 2005. The NJSEA at that point had roughly $800 to $900 million of total outstanding debt.

The Giants and the Jets financed the deal with $650 million each of corporate project revenue bonds to help finance the stadium and loans from the NFL in the amount of $300 million. The NJSEA issued $20.4 million of tax-exempt state contract bonds to help finance the acquisition of twenty-seven acres of land to house the Jets' new practice facilities in Florham Park, which was part of the deal to include the Jets in the project.

By 2010, the new stadium—at a cost of $1.6 billion with an eighty-two-thousand-seat capacity, two hundred suites and ten thousand club seats—opened its doors. The teams also included in their master plan more than 600,000 square feet that is yet to be built. The teams proposed to include in the space team stores; football-themed dining; and club/banquets, entertainment, retail and conference spaces.

Just prior to the stadium issue, the sports authority sought bids from private racetrack owners who might have interest in purchasing the Meadowlands Track and Monmouth Park, which the authority had purchased many years before. Outside financial advisers were hired to assist the boards in their decision. Proposals came in the neighborhood of $300 million. Among the bidders were Churchill Downs, home of the Kentucky Derby, and Magna Entertainment, which operates Pamlico Race Course, the home of the Preakness Stakes. The state said no to the proposals. Codey killed the possible sale. His reasoning was the bidders were looking for commitments for future casinos at both racetracks. The Meadowlands Racetrack was closed under the Christie administration and a new privately owned racetrack was built on the complex site by developer Jeff Gural.

Installation of the enormous New York Giants logo on the training center adjacent to MetLife Stadium. *Courtesy of Christopher Schifano and Network Graphic Imaging, LLC.*

In the latest chapter, Governor Christie signed Executive Order 11, which created the New Jersey Gaming, Sports and Entertainment Advisory Commission. The commission was charged with developing solutions to some of the issues surrounding the financial difficulties of the sports authority. Jon Hanson, former chairman of the NJSEA, heads the committee. The commission made several recommendations to the governor, including a plan to divest the New Jersey Sports and Exposition Authority of all responsibilities.

9
RADIO WAVES

In the 1940s, soon after the end of World War II, a New York City–based AM radio station erected a broadcast tower in the New Jersey Meadowlands. At the time, radio stations installed transmitters on the Empire State Building and other Manhattan skyscrapers, which had become crowded and expensive due to the proliferation of radio after the war. It was discovered that the marsh just west of New York City in New Jersey would enhance AM radio transmission because the wet sandy soil served as a great "ground" for an AM antenna system.

Station WEPN AM 1050 was the first New York City radio station to erect a broadcast tower in New Jersey. During the next thirty years, seven towers rising between five hundred and almost eight hundred feet in the air were built between Kearny and South Hackensack. The Meadowlands was a wasteland during that period, so there was little concern regarding the giant unsightly structures that produced one of the densest collections of radio wave activity in the world. The Federal Communications Commission (FCC) required almost constant monitoring of the radio transmitted by the towers. Therefore, small buildings were erected at the base of the towers that housed engineers who were on duty as long as the tower was transmitting. The practice continued until 1970 and was phased out entirely over the next ten years.

The uncrowded Meadowlands soon became the center of AM radio and some television transmission for the entire New York Metropolitan Area. Radio stations included WOR, one of the nation's oldest stations; WOR TV; WINS News Radio, "Give us twenty minutes, and we will give you the

The great Bobby Darin (left), singer and performer ("Mack the Knife," "Beyond the Sea," "Splish Splash," "Dream Lover," "Bill Baily"), appearing on WOR TV's *Joe Franklin Show* in 1971. WOR TV's 760-foot-high broadcast tower was located in North Bergen. *Courtesy of the Meadowlands Regional Chamber of Commerce.*

world"; and WLIB, which began in the 1940s as a classical music station and later, in the 1970s, became the voice of New York's African American community, locating its broadcast studio in Harlem's Hotel Theresa. Other notable stations transmitting from the Meadowlands included WMCA, WNYC and WHTZ 100 (Z100), and longtime easy listening station WPAT AM located its tower west of the Meadowlands. Some of the additional stations that have been located there are WWRL 1600, WQHT 97FM,

The Z100 Morning Zoo team, circa 1988. *Left to right*: Ross Brittain, John Bell, a visitor and Scott Shannon. The radio station's broadcast tower is one of the oldest in the Meadowlands. *Courtesy of the Meadowlands Regional Chamber of Commerce.*

WSNR, WBLS 107.5FM, Chanel 47 (a cable television station broadcasting NBA and Major League Baseball games) and WNYW TV.

While AM radio was transmitted from lower Bergen County beginning in the 1940s, the northern part of the county was actually the place where FM radio began. In the 1980s, FM radio gained great popularity because of its clear high-fidelity sound, which was especially important to listeners of radio music of all sorts. Major Edwin Armstrong, an electrical engineer and an officer in the U.S. Army's Signal Corps, invented FM radio in the 1930s. Armstrong worked for RCA, the early producer of radio and later television shows, especially over its NBC stations. This relationship led to lawsuits over radio patents, but Armstrong is acknowledged as the father of FM radio.

Major Armstrong resided in Yonkers, New York, in one of the elegant Victorian mansions found in that city's western section high above the Hudson River. The view from the lemonade porch surrounding three sides of the home took in the New Jersey Hudson Palisades that rose majestically above the river on the westerly side. In 1937, Armstrong purchased a small plot of land in Alpine, New Jersey, on the Palisades. The land was about thirty-seven miles from the center of the Meadowlands, where he built the first FM radio station (W2XMN), along with a 425-foot tower, which transmitted radio clearly for one hundred miles, a great innovation at the time.

Armstrong's transmitter is still in use in Alpine. Radio station WFDU 89.1FM—the pioneering radio station operated by Fairleigh Dickinson University since 1971, first in Rutherford and later in Teaneck—transmits from the Armstrong Tower, which also provides directional radio services. Carl Kraus, the former general manager of WFDU and the individual credited with developing the station's well-known ethnic music programming, has felt a connection to Major Armstrong throughout his own storied career in FM radio. "The FM radio people are just different. We love the history of FM radio as much as the current broadcasting. Even with all of the amazing electronic technology available, FM radio remains a powerful media and communications platform," noted Kraus in a recent magazine interview.

Even with his great success and international recognition for his inventions, Armstrong suffered from depression and anxiety. He was wealthy, but his only extravagance seemed to be the purchase of a 1922 Hispano-Suiza motorcar, one of the world's most iconic automobiles, which were manufactured in Barcelona, Spain. He drove the car until 1954, when he took his own life, possibly due to the stress of lawsuits for patent infringement.

Presently, in the Meadowlands, WADO 1280AM broadcasts from a studio on the old Paterson Plank Road behind MetLife Stadium. WADO originally began broadcasting in New York City in the 1920s. In 1927, WADO was the first station to offer local news and reports of happenings around Manhattan using volunteer reporters who witnessed the events and called them into the station using the early telephone system. WADO's broadcast format today is entirely Spanish-language programming.

The transmitters located in the Meadowlands were so important to broadcasters that in 2005 the Infinity Broadcasting Corporation sued the New Jersey Meadowlands Commission, claiming that an amendment to the EnCap Golf project would adversely impact radio transmissions of AM stations owned by Infinity Broadcasting and Inner City Broadcasting Corporation. The project plan included golf courses, a hotel and residential buildings. By adding office towers to the project, radio wave experts claimed that radio transmission would be blocked, greatly reducing the value of the AM stations. The broadcasters lost in court but actually won the day because the EnCap project was later abandoned due to financing issues brought on by the country's financial crises.

George Meade, helicopter pilot, broadcasted over WOR radio for twenty-five years beginning in 1968. WOR began broadcasting from Bamberger's department store in Newark in 1922. *Courtesy of the Meadowlands Regional Chamber of Commerce.*

Due to advances in electronic technology, there is less use for giant radio towers but more use for cellular towers located in service areas. Three of the five-hundred-foot radio towers adjacent to the Izod Center and MetLife Stadium were removed recently by the developer of American Dream, the theme park that will replace the troubled Xanadu. Radio's place in the history of the Meadowlands is assured through publications and online references. Radio and its long and important influence on culture is another one of the pieces that make up the complex Meadowlands tapestry.

10

THE MALLS AND THE MEADOWLANDS

Berry's Creek Center

The 1970 Meadowlands Master Plan envisioned a special area centrally located in the district that would include a retail/commercial, residential, office and transportation hub that would be the focal point of development. The area was called Berry's Creek Center (BCC), almost two hundred acres, located in Rutherford and East Rutherford. As a point of reference, the site is to your right when you cross the bridge on Route 3 eastbound directly across from the sports complex. The BCC master plan broke out the land uses as follows: fifty acres as the main business area, one hundred acres of high-density residential and fifty acres of office space. The master plan describes BCC as a development that would be

> *modern and attractive, embodying the most farsighted architectural concepts. The area will contain a series of plazas of varying size, around and through which the life of the community would flow. Built along the water and next to a Transportation Center, it will be accessible by all forms of transportation including water transit. The center should have all the charm of Venice's San Marco Plaza. It will be the focal point in the changed perception of the Meadowlands.*

In 1978, an application for the project was submitted, and in 1979, it was approved by the Hackensack Meadowlands Development

Commission. The project was led by a management group representing 80 percent of the land area of the Berry's Creek Center zone. The group was Bergen County Associates, owned by H. Jerome Sissleman, who was a landowner and developer in the Meadowlands. They called him the "King of the Meadowlands" for the real estate empire he amassed out of garbage dumps and marshland and the ambitious dreams he nurtured for property that most considered worthless. The applicant proposed 1.8 million square feet of regional shopping center space. There was another 325,000 square feet of commercial, recreational and cultural space proposed to be used for entertainment, restaurants, theaters, exhibition halls, art galleries and performing arts facilities. The plan included a one-thousand-room hotel with 10,000 square feet of meeting space; 3.15 million square feet of office space to be located closest to Route 3; 150,000 square feet of industrial office space, today known as flex space, at the terminus of Murray Hill Parkway; and a total of 3,800 housing units. Included in the housing were 420 low-rise units, 1,198 dwellings in mid-rise buildings and 2,182 units located in high-rise development. About 10 percent of the units were to be set aside for low- and moderate-income households. Approximate unit breakdown was 8 percent studio, 30 percent one bedroom, 38 percent two bedroom and 24 percent three bedroom.

Berry's Creek Center at completion was to be an approximately $700 million development with over half (approximately $398 million) to be completed in Stage 1. Roughly $615 million of the total value would be developed in East Rutherford, with the remaining $69 million in Rutherford. These amounts were all in 1978 dollars. The project called for 9,575 off-site parking spaces at the New Jersey Sports and Exposition Authority parking lots to complete the overall requirements for parking. A people-mover system was proposed that would run through the project site from the Transportation Center and also to the sports complex. The people mover was to be used by patrons going to the stadium and the arena. In return, the sports authority would allow for parking on their site to accommodate both office and shopping center employees. The people mover was also seen as a vehicle to accommodate other future venues at the sports complex and would be expanded as needed using the mass transit hub at Berry's Creek Center. It was also hoped the state would see the value of moving a proposed project in Secaucus that would allow direct one-seat rides into New York City and to Newark.

It was a location where many of the state's rail lines came together at what is now known as Lautenberg Rail Station. One of the transportation consultants for Bergen County Associates was Richard Ravitch, who went on to lead the New York State Urban Development Corporation and Metropolitan Transportation Authority and was the chief owner representative in labor negotiations for Major League Baseball and later Lieutenant Governor of New York.

In its initial approval of the project in 1979, the commission declared Berry's Creek Center as the downtown of the Hackensack Meadowlands District. A report issued by the New Jersey Meadowlands Commission read:

> *Its location at the center of the District and astride the District's major rail and highway links as well, give the Berry's Creek Center its regional economic possibilities. Yet another component of the BCC land use mix—the commercial component—provides a substantial number of semi-skilled jobs that match closely at high employment densities, the job needs in the immediate region. An additional impact of that component is its capacity to provide the kind of economic mix and social attraction which holds together this type of new town center. The stores, shops, restaurants and hotels are all incorporated to attract and capture the office employment component of the development, to the extent that it integrates this variety of uses, is central to the positive economic benefits that can flow from this commercial sector.*

A view of Manhattan from DeKorte Park in Lyndhurst. *Courtesy of the New Jersey Meadowlands Commission.*

The Dream Ends

On August 20, 1980, H. Jerome Sisselman passed away. It was the beginning of the end of the Berry's Creek Center project. With his death, the dream of the "downtown of the Meadowlands" also came to an end. A series of lawsuits and legal maneuvering between the sisters, brother, mother and other partners and a court-appointed trustee lasts even today with their descendants.

Bergen County Associates was formed in 1952. The partnership agreement was amended from time to time, the last being made on December 22, 1977. Prior to Jerome's death, the partners and their respective interests were as follows: Jerome, 8.254 percent; Jerome's wife, Lorraine, 8.254 percent; Sisselman Trust for the Benefit of Lorraine, 20.060 percent; Jerome's son, Selig, and Selig's wife, Deanna, 5.036 percent; S.J. and D.K. Sisselman Trust, 4.000 percent; Helene Goldfinger and her son, Alexander M. Goldfinger Jr., 25.300 percent; and Samuel G. Blumenfeld and his wife, Florence, 9.036 percent. Jerome's death created various issues, such as the dissolution or continuation and management of certain partnerships in which Jerome had an interest, among which were Bergen County Associates (BCA) and Sisselman Israel Associates (SIA). These two partnerships owned the bulk of land in the Berry's Creek Center project that was approved by the Hackensack Meadowlands Commission.

In June 1980, about two months before Jerome died; the SIA and the BCA executed an agreement with Rose Associates, the large New York City developer of Roosevelt Island in New York's East River, for the joint development of the Berry's Creek Center project. In court papers, Selig Sissleman argued that the BCA and SIA agreements should be construed to prevent dissolution of those partnerships notwithstanding the death of Jerome. Alternatively, he contended that even if the partnerships were dissolved, the managing partners designated in the BCA and SIA partnership agreements should continue as managing partners. As such, he urged the trial court to invalidate action taken by Jerome's daughters and the Blumenfeld and Goldfinger interests in reconstituting the BCA partnership and, as successor partners with aggregate interests exceeding 50 percent of BCA, in voting to designate Blumenfeld and Goldfinger as the sole managing partners of BCA, stripping Selig and his mother of their previous managerial authority.

Jerome's daughters supported the dissolution of the BCA, the "reconstitut[ion]" of a new partnership to continue the BCA's business and the majority vote of the new partners having control. During oral arguments at the trial, their position with respect to the SIA was that there be no successor partnership because the successor partners did not reconstitute the partnership. The attorneys for the Goldfingers and Blumenfelds insisted that the death of Jerome and, upon the termination of the trust, the admission of Jerome's daughters into partnership with the surviving partners of the BCA caused the dissolution of the BCA. They contended that upon Jerome's death, the "new and surviving partners" of the BCA were obligated to form a reconstituted partnership. The court agreed with the sisters.

The legal wrangling continued to get worse. Rose Associates claimed it had a valid contract that it wanted to have signed by the HMDC, which insisted that as part of the conditions of approval, it needed to have documents submitted showing ownership. The commission extended the timetable to provide the proofs required, and at each commission meeting, both sides insisted they were close to compromise in order to let the project move forward.

In 1982, the court appointed Arthur Anderson, LLP, at the time a "Big Five" accounting firm, first to appraise the properties to determine their value and then as trustee. The firm was then

> *to negotiate with developers, regulatory authorities, lending institutions, and others as may be deemed necessary for the development of Berry's Creek Center in consultation with the current managers of the entities involved, and only on court approval, enter into development contracts for the sale, lease or other disposition of the land involved in the Berry's Creek development.*

James Wheat, the trustee for Arthur Anderson, did get an offer from Rose Associates, that the court never approved. Another attempt for development by JD Construction developers of the International Plaza in Mahwah to gain control of the site also ended up in court and was turned down.

In a tax court case that made history in the Meadowlands and beyond, called the Crabtree Decision, the court determined Berry's Creek Center's value was not based on the zoning designation of the HMDC but rather the likelihood of getting the necessary federal permits for filling wetlands on the site. When the project was initially approved by the HMDC in 1978, the Army Corps of Engineers and other federal agencies were not focused on wetland issues in the Meadowlands. It was the early 1970s, and the corps was talking only about flood control projects in the region. In a decision that cost municipalities millions in revenue, a state tax court changed the way New Jersey's wetlands may be taxed.

Judge David E. Crabtree ruled that because federal and state regulations restrict the development of wetlands, the tract must be taxed as undevelopable land and not on the basis of its potential commercial value. Judge Crabtree reduced the assessed value from $20 million to under $1 million. The judge found it probable that for most of the property the Army Corps of Engineers could be expected to strictly apply the so-called practical alternatives test under Section 404 of the Clean Water Act. He declared that from 1985 to October 1, 1989, the corps could grant no permits for commercial development in the Meadowlands. Judge Crabtree's ruling resulted in a tremendous loss of tax revenue, which had a large impact on East Rutherford.

In December 1997, the Meadowlands Commission purchased 220 acres of the site for $1.8 million for the purpose of keeping the site as open space in perpetuity and restoring the wetlands. The Sisselman project was derailed by feuding that led to at least ten lawsuits. The feud ended the dream of a downtown center for the Meadowlands. The original renderings from the project are still on the walls of the Meadowlands Commission offices.

Kajima

Kajima, a Tokyo based company, and its co-developer partner Simon Property Group, a major developer of premium shopping malls nationally and in Canada, announced in 1996 that it wished to move forward with a plan to develop a 1.1-million-square-foot project that would focus on entertainment and retail uses. The Meadowlands Entertainment Pavilion included a theme park, indoor skiing, boating, a simulated rain forest the size of a football field within a 90-foot atrium and virtual mountain biking, along with retail. The development would have four entertainment zones, including a twenty-screen cinema. Kajima and Simon would fund the entire $265 million project, and the only thing the state had to do would be to relocate Route 120. Route 120 split the arena area from the rest of the complex. The relocation of the road would move the highway around the arena. This would make fifty-five acres available for the project and would allow for easier access among the various venues at the complex.

The total cost of moving the road was approximately $95 million. Design work for relocating the one-and-a-half-mile road was completed in 1995. The North Jersey Transportation Planning Authority voted to allocate the funds for the relocation project on its five-year list of priority projects. It was estimated it would take three years to build the partially elevated road.

As part of the agreement, the sports authority would share a percentage of the revenue, which some calculated to be approximately $350 million per year. The sports authority would lease the fifty-five acres of land on which Kajima would build the pavilion, which in turn would lease space to commercial tenants.

After the announcement, mayors from the surrounding communities expressed their opposition to the project, citing traffic and impacts to their downtown areas. Kajima officials predicted the site would bring in ten million visitors annually compared to the three and a half million that currently went to the complex. Mayor James Cassella of East Rutherford said the project would only add to the town's traffic problems. "I don't see how this area can handle any more developments of the size you're talking about here," he said. "They don't really care about the people who live here."

Governor Whitman praised the public-private partnership between the sports authority and Kajima. "I think that's a wonderful way to proceed," Whitman said. "But it's got to be looked at in terms of the impact on the region…It's just the beginning. It's an unveiling of an idea. But as far as the initial unveiling goes…those dollars are coming from the private sector."

By January 1997, the contractor was ready to start on the road and was held up because the sports authority did not brief the teams—the Giants, the Jets and the Nets—using the complex. There was concern that up to 1,700 parking spaces could be temporarily lost during construction. The teams were not happy about not being notified, and the Giants were concerned that it would cause problems on game days between the loss of parking and impacts on ingress and egress to the site. John Mara said the Giants would go to court if necessary if the relocation would make it difficult for the fans to enter and leave the stadium. "Those are our concerns. If we determine that it's going to have a negative effect, we'll be opposed to the project," he said. Michael Rowe, president of the New Jersey Nets, said his team supported the project unless it was going to mean losing a big chunk of its 4,000 parking spaces. "I'm a huge fan of the idea, but I also need to be concerned about 600,000 people who try to come to Nets games each year," he said. "Until we can be comfortable we can protect their arrival patterns. We have to insist we be part of the planning process."

Adding to the teams concerns and threats, the Borough of Carlstadt filed suit against the developers, the sports authority and the New Jersey Department of Transportation to stop the development. The papers filed in superior court said that Kajima had a conflict because the sports authority hired a subsidiary of the company to assist on the development of a master plan for the site. The sports authority was supporting the project because the decline in revenues at the complex were causing a deficit, and the sports authority tricked the Department of Transportation to revamp Route 120 on the pretext of needed traffic safety and better flow instead of using the funds for the benefit of private developers. The suit accused the sports authority and the developer of ignoring federal laws on the protection of wetlands.

Kajima withdrew the proposal when the state didn't move forward on moving Route 120. With all the controversy surrounding the move and the litigation, the funds for the project were used to build the tunnel off the Atlantic City Expressway to open an exit for the marina casinos and hotels. Leading the charge to get state funds was Donald Trump.

11

MEADOWLANDS TOWN CENTER/ MEADOWLANDS AND MILLS CORPORATION

Not too far down the road from the Kajima location, Empire Limited of Wood Ridge was proposing a $1 billion mega development called Meadowlands Town Center on what was designated in the master plan as Island Residential development in Carlstadt. The development called for a mall of approximately two million square feet, 5,800 residential units, hotels and three million square feet of office space. The plan almost mirrored the Berry's Creek Center development. Empire Limited's principal partner was Anthony Dinallo of Terminal Construction Company, the builder of the Brendan Byrne Arena. He purchased the property in the 1950s in a deal that was made at the counter of the Bendix Diner. During the '70s and '80s, the company submitted several proposals to the HMDC. The sports authority also looked at the site when George Steinbrenner threatened to leave the Bronx for a new baseball stadium. In 1987, Empire submitted a mixed-use proposal that would have included 4,500 housing units. Those plans were withdrawn to make way for the Meadowlands Town Center proposal. In 1988, the HMDC rezoned the tract to permit large-scale housing and commercial development. The previous zoning was for residential use only. Most of the site is classified as wetlands, and its development called for almost 206 acres of wetlands fill. The balance of the 587-acre site was going to be used to mitigate the wetland impact.

The project received a preliminary approval of the HMDC but still needed two more levels of approval from the commission. For these specially planned areas, the commission would empanel hearing officers consisting of the mayor of the town, two commissioners, the executive director of the commission and the chief engineer. The mayor of Carlstadt at the time was Dominick Presto, who served as mayor for twenty-four years. He was a very influential force in Bergen County politics. After the vote for the preliminary approval of the project, the commissioners asked the mayor if he wished to abstain or vote no and said that the other hearing officers would be fine with his decision because of the potential political ramifications of building 5,800 new units of housing, bringing approximately an additional 18,000 residents into a community with a total population of 5,500. The mayor felt comfortable that he could convince the town that the size of the ratable would reduce their taxes to such an extent that they would support his decision. In the next election for mayor, council president Will Roseman decided to run against Mayor Presto using the overdevelopment card against the incumbent. He made a videotape and distributed it to every voter's home and portrayed (in black and white) areas of the Bronx with public housing, with the voice in the background saying, "Do you want this to happen in Carlstadt?" Presto lost the election.

Enter the Mills Corporation

In 1994, Empire Limited brought a partner into the project, the Mills Corporation. Mills was a Washington, D.C.–based company specializing in developing large outlet-style malls. Its properties were typically between 1.5 million and 1.9 million square feet, five to seven times larger than the typical outlet mall. It had owned and operated malls in Florida, Washington, Philadelphia and Chicago. "The characteristics of the New Jersey/New York area provide us with the opportunity to develop a truly unique project," said Laurence Siegel, Mills chairman and chief executive, upon announcing the agreement. Based on square footage, the mall at that time was going to be the fifth-largest in the country after Mall of America in Bloomington, Minnesota; the Del Amo Fashion Center in Torrance, California; the South Coast Plaza/Crystal Court in Costa Mesa, California; and the Lakewood Center Mall in Lakewood, California. All this was being announced while the $265 million Kajima retail and entertainment center was slated for the sports complex.

The idea of filling 311 acres—reduced to 206 acres and, at the end, to 90 acres—of wetlands for the purpose of building a mall infuriated the environmental community. They had positioned themselves with the cause that the Meadowlands were the last of the urban estuaries left in the New York/New Jersey Metropolitan Area. Even though the Empire Tract might have been behind berms and dikes dating back to the WPA days to eradicate mosquitoes, building the mall would require filling federally protected wetlands, a move the environmentalists strongly opposed. The battle lines were drawn between the development community and the environmental groups. The environmental groups said sacrificing some wetlands to save others violates federal environmental policy. "One of our biggest fears here is that this would set a national precedent that would essentially put public trust wetlands up for sale to finance other schemes," said Andrew Willner, who was director of New York/New Jersey Baykeeper, an environmental group and one of the most vocal opponents of development in the Meadowlands. "We don't think the case law nor does the moral code allow for that," said Bill Sheehan, a resident of Secaucus who attended every public hearing on the matter and organized groups for the sake of battling the mall project. He put together an organization called Hackensack Riverkeeper, which is still going strong today, that devoted itself to this cause and formed a strong bond with Wilner and his group for the fight, as well as attracted other local groups to the cause. The group also enlisted Robert Kennedy Jr., along with the Rutgers Law Clinic, as an ally.

On the other side of the argument, the Mills Corporation hired the most powerful lobbying firms, consultants and attorneys—both in New Jersey and Washington, D.C.—to get the federal and state approvals needed to get the project built. The team included Ann Richards, former Democratic governor of Texas; Robert K. Dawson, former assistant secretary of the army; and Hazel Frank Gluck, Governor Whitman's former campaign co-chairwoman, among others. The Mills Company did not spare any expense to get the project approved. (The facts of what steps Mills would take to get the approvals were brought to light during the trial of Joseph Ferriero, former Bergen County Democrat chairman.) When the project's footprint was reduced and the housing was taken, the mayor of Carlstadt—who opposed the project during his campaign against the incumbent mayor, who initially supported the project—gave his tentative acceptance of the development. The corporation's position was that the wetlands on the site were degraded and of little or no value. It was a philosophy and approach that was shared by the HMDC.

A surprising move by Governor DiFrancesco was his public announcement at the Meadowlands Commission offices that he would oppose the development of this project in the wetlands. The DiFranceso announcement caught everyone off guard. Representatives of Mills immediately asked for a meeting with the governor and their lobbying/public relation teams went into overdrive to minimize the damage. The environmental groups were also in shock. DiFrancesco was looking for an opportunity to gain support from the groups for his run for governor. He was also looking to the bigger picture of allowing development on the sports complex site. This project, if approved, would have destroyed any opportunity at the complex.

The permitting process took almost five years and a federal environmental impact statement prepared by the Army Corps of Engineers (ACE). The Army Corps of Engineers received thousands of letters in favor of and against the project. Joe Seebode of the ACE characterized the comments as "substantial concerns raised by the public, environmental organizations and federal resource agencies that are going to take a substantial effort on our part and The Mills Corporation to address." One of the biggest issues with the other federal agencies, especially the EPA, was the mitigation plan proposed by Mills. The EPA said the plan included nothing more than drainage ponds and did not do anything to restore ecological values. Hackensack riverkeeper Bill Sheehan told the *Bergen Record*:

> *We submitted a couple of hundred pages of testimony, part of that testimony was to let them know that if they issued a permit we were going to take action to stop it, which we can do under the Clean Water Act and the National Environmental Policy Review Act. We've unsheathed our sword in public on more than one occasion and now we've got the EPA backing up the ideas we've expressed.*

The ACE's environmental impact statement found that there would be little significant impact on the environment if the mall were built and 380 acres of wetlands restored. None of those areas would suffer a negative effect if the Mills project went forward, the report stated. Furthermore, the study stated that habitats for wildlife and plant life would actually improve with the restoration of the 380 acres proposed by the original plan. The ACE studied other potential sites. The sites included landfills and some of the land now occupied by the Meadowlands Sports Complex, including the Continental Airlines Arena. Environmental attorney Robert F. Kennedy Jr.—founder of the Water Keeper Alliance, a nonprofit organization committed to the enforcement of the federal Clean Water Act—called the Army Corps' decision "nothing short of a national disaster," in a press release. What was worse for the environmental groups was the fact that Mills had compromised with the HMDC to reduce the site of the wetland impact to 90 acres. A predominate question remained: what project would they try to build now?

Another controversy that arose during this period of regulatory review was the fact that Mills executives and their families donated $150,000 to state and federal candidates, including $43,000 to Vice President Al Gore's presidential election campaign. Gore was the chairman of the Council on Environmental Quality (CEQ) in the White House, which was reviewing the project, and the Special Area Management Plan. Larry Siegel, CEO of the Mills Corporation, stood on stage with President Clinton at a school in Newark when the president announced that Mills was pledging to hire one thousand Newark residents to work at Meadowlands Mills.

Environmentalists said that donations from Mills executives and their families to Gore's presidential campaign were a blatant attempt to influence federal officials who were considering the company's request to fill in up to 206 acres of wetlands. Mills officials said there was no connection between the donations and the project.

A Special Area Management Plan

During this time period, the Hackensack Meadowlands Development Commission was working on a Special Area Management Plan (SAMP) with the Army Corps of Engineers, the EPA, the NJDEP and the National Oceanic and Atmospheric Administration (NOAA). The U.S. Fish and Wildlife Service was asked to participate but did not sign the Memorandum of Understanding with the other agencies. The idea was to align the master plan with all federal and state environmental laws and regulations that were adopted after 1970, the year the Meadowlands Master Plan was adopted. The SAMP goal was to use the plan as a guide for the ACE and EPA to administer Section 404 of the Clean Water Act, which is related to filling wetlands. It allowed 845 acres to be filled and preserved the remaining 7,500 acres of wetlands and waterways. From the commission's perspective, it was the only way of breaking the regulatory logjam.

In the Meadowlands, it was becoming a reality that wetland fill permits for development were becoming more and more difficult to get. Some projects were taking between five and ten years to get through the permitting process of the federal and state agencies. Many times, a developer just gave up and others filed suit declaring that the federal government had, in effect, confiscated property without proper compensation, also called inverse condemnation of property. Hartz Mountain attempted to get permits for a two-thousand-unit development in the north end of Secaucus and went through a ten-year process only to abandon the project.

The Westway project, which would have filled seven hundred acres of the New York shoreline, was the defining event that added to the more stringent approach of the federal agencies in the interpretation of Section 404 of the Clean Water Act. In 1981, President Reagan and the Army Corps of Engineers were on board for the construction of the project. The main issues were the validity of the environmental impact statement and the procedures followed by the corps. The issuance of the permit was challenged and blocked in federal district court, and the U.S. Court of Appeals upheld that decision.

The Meadowlands SAMP land uses were also tested through an environmental impact statement, which included the Empire Tract site as one of the growth centers, albeit at a lower wetlands impact. Potential SAMP development was going to be the basis of a program that would place impact fees on the development for the purpose of generating enough revenue to offset the cost of environmental improvement throughout the Meadowlands, which totaled almost $800 million.

Bradley Campbell, an associate director of the CEQ and later NJDEP commissioner, met with all parties involved in the SAMP. He was looking for a solution and to find common ground on the SAMP. His biggest fear was that the Reagan-appointed federal judges would start siding with developers who would claim a "taking" of their property. It was felt by CEQ that the SAMP could be the long-term approach to find a balance between protection of wetlands and economic development. Campbell did get concessions. He reduced the wetland fill outlined in the SAMP by more than half and secured a hard commitment on the mall project to ninety acres. When the new wetlands fill numbers were outlined in the Federal Register, the mall project received the concession of not requiring further studies for alternative upland sites. This was a big concession that could make or break any project involving wetlands.

With the U.S. Fish and Wildlife Service's continued opposition to the SAMP and with a new change in governor from DiFrancesco to Jim

McGreevey, the SAMP effort ended after fourteen years. It did not end the outstanding issue of the Mills wetlands fill permit application. The stage was now set for another shift.

Xanadu

New Jersey Community Affairs commissioner Susan B. Levin, the New Jersey Department of Environmental Protection commissioner Bradley M. Campbell and sports authority head George Zoffinger sent a letter to the ACE, saying that the ACE should either reevaluate the proposed development in Carlstadt "or deny the permit forthwith." The letter also urged the ACE to consider the "authority site as a viable alternative." Mills had shown it might be interested. The State of New Jersey presented a huge roadblock to the ACE by offering an upland alternative to filling in any wetlands for mall development.

With that in the way, Mills had no choice but to look at the potential of development on the sports complex site. Before it could do that, a request for proposals had to be submitted to the sports authority, which was opened to everyone that had an interest in developing the area adjacent to the arena. The authority received proposals from Hartz, Westfield, the owners of Garden State Mall, International Speedways and Triple Five LLC. The field was narrowed to Mills, Hartz and Westfield. Emmanuel Stern, after the announcement, told the *Bergen Record* that he promised that his direct-mail campaign would "hit everyone over the head" with the difference between the Hartz/Forest City Ratner plan and a rival plan (Mills) that, he said, "cannibalizes the existing environment" and "rains a corrosive effect on the region."

All three proposals included 2.0 million square feet of office, but the Mills' "Xanadu" plan called for a total of 4.8 million square feet of development that included 1.5 million square feet of sports and entertainment—or, as the Mills CEO Larry Spiegel called it, "shoppertainment." The retail uses in the Mills project was almost twice the amount of the other submissions. The opponents of Xanadu used its retail size as an avenue of attack, pointing out that it would have a damaging effect on existing malls and local stores in the surrounding municipalities.

The sports authority selected Mills as the best proposal and started the process of negotiating leases and conditions of development. The $1.3 billion entertainment and shopping center on the 104-acre site called for a lease payment of $160 million. Needless to say, an agency that was in financial distress was looking for that payment. The unique feature of the Mills submission was the donation of the 587-acre Empire Tract to the State of New Jersey. The plan called for the site to be given to the Meadowlands Conservation Trust, which was created as a land conservancy agency that was in but not of the Meadowlands Commission. The initial reports of the donation were that Mills was going to improve the wetlands on the site prior to giving it to the state. What everyone did not realize was that the real proposal was to convert the Empire Tract into a wetland mitigation bank. The mitigation bank was going to be able to sell credits to developers that were filling in wetlands in the Meadowlands. It was anticipated that the site would be turned over to the state in ten years. This became a problem for the state inasmuch as it would be a public relations nightmare to be involved with a project that would assist filling wetlands. It was anticipated that Mills could make up to $60 million in selling the credits. That forced the sports authority to adjust the lease payment.

As with every project at the sports complex, the NJDEP and the Meadowlands Commission conducted hearings on the development. The lobbying effort was intense. The unions were mobilized; the plan promised a YMCA; there was going to be a location for a Bergen County Community College campus; a minor-league baseball park was going to be built for the Bergen County Cliffhawks by Steve Kalafer, a well-known entrepreneur in the state; and twenty-five thousand jobs were going to be created. Mills was very sensitive to the number of public hearings that were held in this process because every time there was a hearing, the stock would go down. Traffic was a big issue, as it always was at the complex.

The recommendations made by the hearing officers included additional traffic studies, making sure green building principles were used and that revenue be generated through parking surcharges to help offset costs to address infrastructure needs in the region. Mills was successful in setting aside several of these recommendations because, in the company's view, the additional costs would be prohibitive. The idea of Steve Kalafer getting the minor-league stadium went by the wayside, as did the YMCA and the college when the approvals were given. Kalafer's litigation and the production of a film called *The Soprano State: New Jersey's Culture of Corruption* was symbolic for the frustration of what was promised and what was reneged just to get local and county politicians and leaders on board. Examples of bait and switch were everywhere. The McGreevy administration wanted this project as a centerpiece in the next reelection bid, especially related to job creation, and was not going to push back too hard when Mills officials said they would not do the project with all these conditions and elements. While Mills contributed $67 million to infrastructure, the definition was very broad and included water and sewer extensions to the development. At the end of the day, the state—through the NJDOT, the New Jersey Turnpike and the Port Authority of New York and New Jersey—came through with considerable money for new ramps and roads and a rail line into the complex site.

Hartz, which was not going away without a fight, filed suit against Mills and the sports authority alleging the selection of Mills was cloaked in "secrecy, favoritism and unfairness," and said it was going to stop the project. The suit also contended that the amount of retail space in Xanadu was not permitted under the sport authority enabling legislation. The suit also included deficiencies in the environmental impact statement, possible violations of the state Open Public Meetings Act and the transfer of the Empire Tract as an "unfair and improper competitive disadvantage."

Hartz did win the issue that it had a right to documents held by the sports authority, but on every other count in its lawsuits, the courts did not agree with Hartz. The interesting aspect to all of this was the remaking of the Hartz's Harmon Meadow retail complex in Secaucus during the lawsuits and legal maneuvering. The company was able to add big box retail components, restaurants, new movie theaters and hotels. These changes proved to be very lucrative for the former pet food giant. It was able to modernize and add to its properties during the legal battles.

Xanadu started construction in 2005 with its ugly color scheme. It was brought before the sports authority board to discuss the color scheme only to be told by Mills officials and architects that the colors drew attention to the site. By 2007, Mills was collapsing under a heavy debt load that put the company on the verge of bankruptcy. Compounding the problem was a U.S. Securities and Exchange Commission filing that detailed an internal audit showing accounting errors and possible executive misconduct. In another step toward solving its problems, the Mills Corporation entered into an agreement with Colony Capital and Kan Am USA Management for construction financing. This move took control of the project from Mills to Colony. Colony Capital and its partners took over Xanadu in 2006 from the now-defunct Mills and ran into major financing problems when an affiliate of bankrupt Lehman Brothers stopped providing promised construction funds. Between the Great Recession and the collapse of Lehman, the project slowed and then stopped completely.

Enter Triple Five

Triple Five, owners of Mall of America and the West Edmonton Mall in Canada, acquired the incomplete project from the lenders who owned the debt on the project in 2010 and renamed the project American Dream. One of the conditions of the takeover was that the the outside of the multicolored building, which had been declared the ugliest building in New Jersey, be changed immediately, . A part of the changes to the mall was the construction of an indoor water and amusement park. These new additions required a wetland fill permit. That permit actually was the centerpiece of a congressional primary. Two veteran legislators, Congressmen William Pascrell and Steve Rothman, ended up in the same district as result of redistricting. Both went out of their way to make it their mission to lobby both the Army Corps of Engineers and EPA to approve a permit. Both were vying for labor support. The permits were issued, and Bill Pascrell won the primary. The American Dream project actually had little to do with the election's results. Today, we wait for a complex funding scheme to be put in place in order to start the project back up.

12

FROM TRASH TO TEES AND BACK

The Meadowlands Commission had developed the concept that it could environmentally close landfills in Lyndhurst and Rutherford without financial assistance from the agency coffers by designating a redevelopment area that would allow a golf course, some residential units, a hotel and maybe even a few small office buildings. Little did the staff know that such an idea could so desperately go wrong and would entail an inspector general's investigation, federal probes of the companies involved, political influence at the highest levels, bankruptcy, the loss of approximately $60 million from a state environmental trust fund and several municipal officials being hoodwinked, thinking their towns would be the recipients of tens of millions of dollars.

This project, known as EnCap, spanned several administrations in Trenton and numerous local officials. How it all got started and how it ended were part of the malaise that typified the new millennium, with banks giving loans to everyone, regardless of creditworthiness, and developers' greed with the never-ending ambition to extend and extract more and more even when there was no more to give.

The selection process was a straightforward exercise for the commission, which issued a request for a qualification (RFQ) document looking for companies that might have an interest in undertaking such a project. The project was high risk but could have a high yield of rewards if successful. The commission was interested in looking for a company that was building or had built a golf course on a landfill. The evaluation team consisted of Rutherford and Lyndhurst officials and members of the commission staff, all under with the guidance of the Attorney General's Office. With the review process complete, the leading candidate to be named redeveloper was a company called EnCap Golf Holdings. The company specialized in taking environmentally stressed properties to remediate and develop. It was part of the holdings of an individual named Louis Gonda, president of Lexington Commercial Holdings. Gonda was on the Forbes list of the wealthiest people in the United States.

The response in the RFQ documents stated:

> *EnCap is experienced in developing projects similar to the Meadowlands golf course, as evidenced by the project in Houston. The concept of building golf courses on landfills has been tried by others. Individual courses have been designed and constructed by a number of different developers. Many of these developers have been discouraged by potential environmental liabilities, increased construction and maintenance costs, and technical uncertainties. EnCap's unique business strategy, and that of our strategic alliance partners, is to identify, evaluate, and secure closed landfill properties that are suitable for redevelopment as golf courses on a national basis: making us the first true "brownfield" golf course developer. Our strategic vision is confirmed on a regular basis as public and private site owners approach EnCap to convert their properties into golf course developments.*

The company also made it clear in its submission that:

> *EnCap will secure private funds to develop the project. This private funds approach will significantly expedite the project. To reduce the project costs, every attempt will be made to use other State and local financial incentives, tax advantages, financial instruments, and economic benefits available to the developer. However, progress of the project will not be subject to the constraints of tax incentives application reviews, bond issuance process, and third party financial assistance.*

The EnCap proposal received the highest grades based on the fact that it was doing a similar project in Houston, required no financial assistance from the state and had a team of professionals that were experienced in handling the task of landfill closure and reclamation. Right before EnCap was named by the commission as the redeveloper, Gonda dropped out of the equation and was replaced by Cherokee Investment, an equity firm that invested in brownfield development. The new company's sources of investment funds were pension funds and university endowment funds, among others in its portfolio. The question at the time was whether that change was enough to stop the award of an agreement. The commission and its attorneys agreed Cherokee was a solid company with the financial wherewithal to undertake the project. With that change and only that change, EnCap was named redeveloper.

Fore!

Over the next year, the due diligence process was in full swing, and it became apparent that the key component of the financial success of this project was bringing in soils, dredge and other recycled materials that would fill and contour the site for the golf course. These materials would have a value either per ton or cubic yard and could generate millions of dollars to whoever controlled the property. This was happening during the time that there was the need to dredge the navigation channels of the ports. Contracts were being awarded at forty-nine dollars a cubic yard with millions of yards yet to be dredged and disposed in upland locations. The government had banned the ocean dumping of the contaminant dredge.

Attempts by the commission to get the port authority and the Army Corps of Engineers to designate the EnCap development site as the sole depository for dredge were unsuccessful. Alan Steinberg, who was executive director of the commission, led the discussions with those agencies. Neither agency was interested in an intergovernmental agreement because of bidding concerns and potential litigation by dredgers working in the harbor. As part of the plan to bring dredge to the site without trucking, EnCap proposed building a dock at Lyndhurst that would eventually be turned into a marina.

During the due diligence period, EnCap officials came to the commission with the idea that the redevelopment site should be expanded to include the Kingsland Landfill and also the Bergen County Utilities Authority Solid Waste Transfer Station. The State of New Jersey, the commission, the Bergen County Utilities Authority and Bergen County worked out a land transaction that included the acquisition of those properties in exchange for cash, but the deal also included a provision to extinguish the outstanding solid waste stranded debt of Bergen County. The total cost to the commission and state was over $90 million. Legislation was passed to allow this transaction, but that legislation also included changes to the Brownfield Act to allow more expenses to be included to be recouped under the law, including professional services. The commission was also directed to provide funds to the project that would be reimbursed upon the execution of liability policies for closure, which eventually did occur.

To say that EnCap became more and more politically connected was an understatement. The project started with Governor Whitman and ended under Governor Corzine. Each governor and staff were enlisted to provide assistance where possible. The message was clear: in each administration, this project had a very high priority. Even in the legislature, where a bill was needed for the Bergen transaction, the bill was heard on the last day of a legislative session. The committee that heard the bill refused to act on it, thus killing it for that session, but it was resurrected an hour later and released from committee. When the attorney for EnCap, Eric Wisler of the DeCotiis law firm, was asked by the committee if this financial transaction was safe, he told the committee he was absolutely sure. He was so sure that he jokingly said he would reimburse the commission if something happened. The bill was passed by both houses and signed by Governor DiFrancesco on the last day he was governor. Wisler was very good at the divide-and-conquer approach with the state agencies and all the administration in Trenton. Information was doled out in increments and many times the whole story was not given until absolutely necessary.

Eric Wisler was a brilliant attorney and was able to articulate the complex elements of the deal. But he always pushed the envelope to get more and more for his client. It became a feeding frenzy. EnCap was never satisfied with what it received and needed more and more without finishing even the first phase. Somehow, everyone was involved one way or another with EnCap. Soil brokers were making deals with the company, other potential developers were being positioned in the background and promises were being made to local officials, who were used like pawns.

The thought of making a windfall on the fill material was clearly losing ground. EnCap would make money but not to the extent it had hoped. The idea of interval residential units and offices started to lose ground to town houses and condos. The number of units proposed needed the support of the mayors and councils in Lyndhurst and Rutherford. To gain support in those towns, contributions were made to those running for office and to community organizations. Every time EnCap officials needed more units, the towns were promised more and more money in the payment in lieu of taxes (PILOTS) agreements. In some cases, the payments were made upfront to solve local budget shortfalls, which only created future structural deficit in the municipal budgets. Landfill properties that were not remediated were assessed at $300,000 an acre for no apparent reason.

The structure being proposed was a very complex taxing structure that would require the towns to assess the town houses, condos and hotels at a rate higher than anywhere else in the town. That increment would be the basis for the towns to float bonds that would be used toward development costs. All of this was part of separate agreements between EnCap, Rutherford and Lyndhurst. Additionally, EnCap received a $212 million no-interest/low-interest loan commitment from the New Jersey Environmental Infrastructure Trust fund (NJEIT) for the landfill closure work. To get those funds, EnCap had to have a local government sponsor be a conduit for the funds. The Bergen County Improvement Authority was the sponsoring agency. The NJEIT's board and other high-level state officials needed to sign off on the legislation to appropriate the funds. Meetings were had between NJEIT staff and the Meadowlands Commission staff to determine if the commission would provide any collateral for the loans. At that meeting, the answer was no, and the discussion continued as to how the state could give such a large amount without any collateral. It was not long after this that the commission staff was isolated from the NJEIT discussions. Samuel Wolfe, assistant NJDEP commissioner, wrote a memo regarding the EnCap loan, stating, "It will not meet the Financing Program's normal creditworthiness standards."

It was also a period of time in the banking industry that a monkey with a suit could get a loan from a bank. It was true in this case, where several banks, including a Wachovia-led consortium of banks, invested in the project.

Remediation commenced on the site, and questions started to arise as to how remediation was being done. For example, dredge was brought to the site by truck. After the dredge was brought to the site, workers utilized a method called dynamic compaction. Literally, the ground is pounded to compact the soil so that the site can be developed. The one thing EnCap did not take into account was the fact that the underlying soil of the Meadowlands is like a sponge. You can flatten the sponge, but eventually, it will spring back up. This happened time and time again, which required the process to be done over and over again, and more fill had to be used than was anticipated. The project was obviously in trouble when the workers did not even bother to put in internal roads to move equipment around the landfills, and bulldozers got stuck in the mud. EnCap reopened the Kingsland Landfill, disassembled the methane gas recovery system and then left it that way for several years. Kingsland Landfill was deemed to be 98 percent completely environmentally closed when the project started, but at the end, millions of dollars had to be spent to get it back to complete closure.

EnCap pushed the local municipalities to agree to more and more housing units. The company had a contract with a major housing developer, Pulte Homes. Pulte Homes had a $150 million agreement in principle to build 1,980 of the 2,850 homes in the first phase. A spokesperson for Pulte said, "We're moving forward in our efforts to gain approvals and permits required for our contribution to this project—the residential construction phase, which we hope to begin as soon as possible after EnCap has completed all remediation work and delivers construction-ready land to us." If you looked at the conditions of the contract, you might wonder if the units would ever be built. If Pulte wasn't going to build the dwellings, there were others waiting to step into its shoes. Eventually, EnCap bought Pulte out of its contract for $8 million.

The Meadowland Commission board started to become weary of the added housing. The commission started to require the local governing body to endorse the additional housing units by resolution. Cherokee Urban Renewal LLC, not EnCap, won a bid to secure a 45.6-acre tract in North Arlington that was completely outside the Meadowlands District and not under the control of the commission. The property was originally designated for warehouse space. With this acquisition, Cherokee also wanted to add another private golf course on the 1-E Landfill site. The other courses had to be public courses under the terms of the contract. North Arlington agreed to more housing and received a payment for signing the agreement. A commissioner on the Meadowlands, Leonard Kaiser, the former mayor of North Arlington, warned the commission about agreeing to this expansion of the project. He indicated the commission should wait until the municipality had a final agreement.

Cherokee offered the commission $35 million, and in return, the agency would give up control of a landfill and a solid waste transfer station. The commission, which did not receive any appropriation, looked at the package as very enticing, as did the governor's office that supported the move. The Kaiser warning went unheeded. In the end, he had the privilege to make the motion to kill the overall EnCap agreement for the project inside the Meadowlands District. After the agreement was abandoned by the commission, EnCap declared bankruptcy.

The Meadowlands Commission still had to negotiate with Cherokee on the North Arlington agreement. First, the commission retained the 1-E Landfill, which was not a surprise. Next, it received the rights back on the transfer station so that North Arlington did not lose its host community fees and the right to process its waste for free. These two issues had a significant financial impact on North Arlington. The commission was able to accomplish those goals. At the end of the day, the commission received close to $27 million in land and cash in a settlement with Cherokee. North Arlington went to court after the project collapsed to negate the contract with Cherokee. The court negated the contract, but it also ruled that North Arlington had to pay back the initial payment it received at the time of its signing the contract. This caused the town to pay back the millions and required taxes to be increased.

By the time the project ended in bankruptcy, more than seventeen local officials were voted out of office. The EnCap people promised so much to the towns; and the towns bought the pot of gold at the end of the rainbow that the company was selling. Several times, the commission staff asked to attend meetings to give technical and financial advice to the municipalities only to be disinvited hours before the meetings. In Lyndhurst, EnCap's agreement called for a recreation center and ball fields. The mayor asked if the fields could be turf fields. EnCap agreed only if the mayor would take less money for PILOTS over a thirty-year period. That would have made the field the most expensive field known to man. The mayor tried to put in a resolution to move this concept forward but was defeated at the polls, and the resolution never passed. During that election, EnCap sent to every home in Lyndhurst a flyer describing how much the town was going to receive from the project. What EnCap failed to say was the amount on the campaign piece was a gross amount and not the fraction of the amount the town was going to receive after EnCap bonds were paid.

It became apparent that the insurance policies covering EnCap were not going to be enough. Progress on the closure of the old landfills was moving slowly, and the commission questioned the design. EnCap was being allowed to use plastic sheet piling that was going down maybe twenty feet to contain the leachate from the landfills. The Meadowlands closure method was very different from the commission's approach, which was to surround the landfills with a clay bentonite wall that would go down to the clay layer in the subsurface, thus creating a bathtub. The walls had a leachate collection system that would collect the leachate and send it to a sewer treatment plant. EnCap had leachate collection systems, but they were in such long segments that if there were a break, it would be impossible to find the problem. The EnCap approach was unique but approved by NJDEP.

The commission forced the issue with EnCap to get a performance bond for the closure work. The calculation of the amount of the performance bond was based on 125 percent of the closure costs as approved by NJDEP. As a result, the commission was given a performance bond in the amount of $148.8 million from the American International Group (AIG) that would be used if the closure work was not done by EnCap.

Shortly after the issuance of the performance bond, cracks were starting to show in the financial structure of the deal. There were signs that there were money problems, and eventually, EnCap did acknowledge that the closure of the landfills far exceeded its expectations.

Jeff Pillets and John Brennan wrote a series of articles for the *Record* on EnCap that almost won them a Pultizer Prize. Their reports detailed the politics behind the project and the concessions EnCap received from the state. Pillets wrote in a June 2007 article:

> *In October 2003, Assistant Attorney General Stefanie Brand sent a blistering e-mail to her colleagues describing how EnCap had already reneged on key agreements with the state and was months overdue on $10.5 million in various payments to state agencies. Brand pointed out that EnCap had missed deadlines to use Hudson River dredge as fill to cover the four Meadowlands landfills that make up the project. As a result, she said, the state would be forced to let EnCap cover the old landfills with potentially contaminated recycled material—stuff haulers would normally pay a working landfill to accept. "Allowing EnCap to substitute 'recyclables' for dredge would mean a huge economic windfall for EnCap, less environmental benefit, and could result in criticism due to the concessions DEP made," Brand wrote.*

EnCap eventually told the state that the estimated remediation costs grew to $185 million. Under the terms of the agreement with the commission, EnCap was required to put up additional bonds or collateral to meet the responsibility of putting 125 percent of the cost of closure in case it failed to remediate the landfills. EnCap was told it had to put up an additional $16 million. It failed to come up with the money and was found to have defaulted on the agreements. It declared bankruptcy several months later.

By the end of 2007, Donald Trump had entered into the picture with an agreement with Cherokee Investment Partners to take over the project and get it back on track with the remediation work. On the day before Thanksgiving 2007, late in the afternoon, Trump introduced the team that would be working on the project. The Trump organization agreed to provide to the state a cost estimate of the total remediation costs. The cost estimated to finish closure was approximately $124 million. Governor Corzine agreed to give the Trump organization an opportunity to save the project. Trump was willing to take on the troubled EnCap golf and housing development with a new design, a world-class golf course and more upscale housing. Donald Trump promised a new master plan for the project. After more than a year, the state pulled the plug on the Trump attempt to save the project. The state had insisted that Trump put additional funding into the project, which he refused to do. Trump was not pleased about the decision and lashed out at the state and, in particular, Governor Corzine.

Another individual that was brought on by Cherokee was Jim Dausch, of the failed Mills project fame. He blamed the state for EnCap's problems because the state would not accept the terms of various bailout proposals brought to the U.S. Bankruptcy Court. Some of the proposals included more state money.

In a *Bergen Record* article from May 2008, Brennan described what Dausch (the same Jim Dausch who was a key witness for the federal trial of Joseph Ferriero, former Bergen Democrat chairman, who is under indictment for his role in the Mills project) claimed in his affidavit to the bankruptcy court on how EnCap spent $317 million on project:

- $103 million on landfill remediation
- $22 million on site engineering
- $27 million on land and other acquisition costs ($17 million paid to the New Jersey Meadowlands Commission for the 785-acre project site in Lyndhurst and Rutherford)
- $4 million in property taxes paid to the towns
- $13 million on payments to benefit the communities, including community projects like the recreational center and new ball fields in Lyndhurst
- $7 million on project management
- $6 million on administrative and other costs
- $85 million on interest and finance costs
- $16 million on legal fees

To spend an aggregate total of $317 million for project that was not even close to 30 percent to 40 percent completed on the remediation was a gross miscalculation.

In the meantime, Governor Codey asked the state inspector general Mary Jane Cooper to investigate how this project got to this point. Everyone was interviewed, either by Cooper or her staff. On several occasions, the Meadowlands Commission's staff members were interviewed about the selection process and the agreements. Tens of thousands of pages were turned over, and further discussions were held after interviews of others involved in the project. The staff of the Meadowlands Commission offered the inspector general funds to do a forensic audit of the EnCap books and funds. The proposal was never accepted, which could have answered many questions. It was disappointing that previous governors and their immediate senior staff were not questioned.

The commission sought to call on the $148.8 million performance bond from AIG. AIG refused to act on the bond because it indicated the last agreement between the Meadowlands Commission and EnCap voided previous language when the bond was issued. The Meadowlands issued a press release attacking AIG for its inaction. This was the time of bank meltdowns, and AIG was one of the companies that were in need of a government bailout. When the article came out that AIG was giving millions and millions of dollars in bonuses to executives, the attacks on AIG gained traction. Governor Corzine directed all state agencies and authorities not to award any insurance contract written by AIG. One of the agencies was the Port Authority of New York and New Jersey. Within twenty-four hours, AIG contacted the governor's office, and the bond money was made available.

When the report was issued, the inspector general did go before a state senate committee to testify on the report. The report absolved the mayors and councils of Rutherford and Lyndhurst as innocent bystanders. Upon questioning by the panel, Cooper was hit hard with questions about the incompleteness of the report and why she did not interview former governors and their senior staff. The report offered no insight as to how the project got into this situation. Some thought the report was a whitewash.

What was revealed was the amount of campaign contributions made by EnCap and Cherokee officials. Bill Gauger, president of EnCap and Cherokee Northeast, told the inspector general "that while he did not make contributions with the expectation that they would generate a certain outcome or a particular benefit for the Project, he understood that by making a contribution it could help…to make sure something bad doesn't happen because you were not involved in the political process." Regarding his contribution to Mayor James Guida of Lyndhurst, the report characterized Gauger's May 2001 $2,000 contribution and his June 2005 $4,000 contribution to Guida as "relatively small." At the time of each contribution, Guida was campaigning for reelection as mayor of Lyndhurst.

Gauger also admitted to the office of the inspector general that EnCap did not close the Houston landfill. It was done by others.

In addition to the inspector general's investigation, the U.S. Attorney's Office in New Jersey conducted its own investigation into the matter. Attorney Paul Fishman, the present United States attorney for New Jersey, represented EnCap and Cherokee in both of these investigations.

Federal and state law enforcement officials also investigated potential mob influence in the dumping of materials on the site. The probe centered on whether payoffs were accepted to allow dumping at the site. LIR Fiore had an $8 million contract with EnCap in 2004 to provide two and a half million yards of fill for the Meadowlands project. Leroy Robinson of Maplewood was president of LIR Consulting, which had a 51 percent interest in the subsidiary LIR Fiore. EnCap officials said cost overruns were due to the unexpectedly high cost of fill. LIR Fiore received $13.7 million from the state loan. No charges were ever made against these individuals. It was found out during this investigation that Eric Wisler's wife was put on the payroll of Robinson's company.

In 2010, Wisler and state senator Wayne Bryant were both indicted as a result of the EnCap project and another project in Camden. In 2004, Wisler was accused of entering an $8,000 retainer agreement with Bryant's firm. The payment was allegedly for legal work relating to land use, condemnation and other matters for a development project in the New Jersey Meadowlands. The federal government said the payments were actually bribes paid in exchange for votes Bryant took as chairman of the appropriations committee and as a senator in favor of the redevelopment projects Wisler was involved with, including EnCap and a proposed $1.2 billion redevelopment of Camden's Cramer Hill neighborhood, in which Cherokee was involved.

Specifically, Bryant supported and sponsored legislation to the Redevelopment Area Bond Financing Law that facilitated bond financing for the Meadowlands project and appropriations from which the Meadowlands project received more than $200 million in loans.

Wisler, at this time, had been battling cancer for several years. He succumbed to the disease and never came to trial. Bryant went on trial while he was in prison for another crime and received a bench trial—a trial without a jury—and was found not guilty.

The federal investigation went on for years. The only other indictment that was issued was for Bill Gauger, president of EnCap and Cherokee Northeast, on charges that were not related to the EnCap project. He was given probation and did not serve any time.

More than seventeen years after the concept of closing landfills using private development money from the Meadowlands Commission, the property has been put up for sale for the purpose of building warehouse space on the site. It turned out that the $148.8 million bond was not enough to environmentally remediate all the property; the properties are in a position to be developed with the balance of the environmental work to be done by the developer. It comes at a time when warehouse space in the Meadowlands is at a premium.

What was envisioned to be a creative approach to a serious environmental problem ended up a disaster.

13

FUTURE OF THE MEADOWLANDS

So many people ask the question: after forty-six years of existence, what is next for the Meadowlands region, the Meadowlands Commission and the sports complex? The answer was provided by Governor Christie on February 5, 2015, when he signed a bill sponsored by assembly Speaker Vincent Prieto and state senator Paul Sarlo. The Meadowlands Commission was dissolved and combined into one agency with the New Jersey Sports and Exposition Authority. So the next question you may be asking is how did the commission get dissolved and collapsed into the NJSEA? The answer is very complex.

The New Jersey Meadowlands Commission leadership changed at the end of 2010, when former state senator Marcia Karrow took over the reins of the agency. Marcia Karrow, from Hunterdon County, was promised a position when the Christie administration came into office. The question for the administration was what was the best fit for Karrow, who was known to be an outspoken member of the legislature? She was a member of the assembly and was appointed to the state senate when Leonard Lance was elected to Congress. Karrow lost in a primary to Michael Doherty, so her time in the senate was very short-lived. However, she still likes to be called senator. Karrow requested the job, and when the position of executive director opened up due to retirement, she was designated for the position. As a member of the Christie transition team studying the NJDEP, she was very unpopular with factions in the environmental community. She was also the main figure of a proposed change to the affordable housing laws in the state.

The Robert Ceberio Environmental Education Pavilion, elegantly constructed of natural wood, was dedicated in 2011 to the retiring executive director of the New Jersey Meadowlands Commission by the board of commissioners. The board recognized Ceberio's leadership in improving the knowledge of the environment for over 200,000 school children who participated in programs developed and operated during Ceberio's tenure. *Courtesy of the New Jersey Meadowlands Commission.*

When her coming to the Meadowlands Commission became more imminent, several Bergen County legislators resisted the idea that someone from outside Bergen County would get the job. They lobbied the governor with their own candidate. It was a standoff that was quickly addressed by allowing the Bergen candidate to become deputy executive director of the agency. There was also resistance on the board of commissioners that required the outgoing executive director to lobby the board to get enough votes for the appointment.

A New Leaf

The mayors and the municipalities of the region, over a long period of time, were treated with a tremendous amount of respect, open lines of communications and with a philosophy of assisting the towns in their times of need. For new executive director Karrow, a system and philosophy of command and control was the predominate feature of her management style. That approach impacted relations with the towns. Her responses at a Hackensack Mayor's Municipal Committee (HMMC) on the status of different municipal programs that the commission sponsored was "I'm not Christmas tree Bob," referring to the previous executive director.

Even the staff was subjected to an atmosphere of fear and retribution. That was unfortunate, because the NJMC staff was creative, full of energy and always trying to find new and innovative ways of approaching problems. Many of the previous programs were eliminated as wasteful or brushed off as not part of the core mission of the agency, and blame for any error was placed on others rather than trying to find new approaches or to find the resources to keep programs going that were beneficial for the communities. She portrayed an agency as out of money, even though the agency lent itself $25 million to prepare the Keegan landfill and needed to "hide" funds in reserves to avoid getting raided by the state treasury again. Even Governor Christie was not spared blame when the new executive director pointed to Trenton as the cause when something was eliminated or not done.

Also during this period, the commission lost its long-standing chief financial officer, Irfan Bora, to retirement. Bora was a financial wizard and actually made the commission so successful by managing its finances that the agency was always in a position to pay in cash and did not have one dollar in outstanding debt. Not many public agencies could make that claim. Without his guidance, Karrow blamed everything on the agency's lack of funds and continued to attack previous management for any of the agency's ills. She continued to cut programs, like the very successful Environmental Education Program operated by Ramapo College of New Jersey, which brought over forty thousand students and visitors to the commission's environment center. It was done without looking for new and different funding sources, which was always the way the commission had operated.

This atmosphere established by Karrow led to immediate clashes with mayors, in particular, Mayor Michael Gonnelli of Secaucus. Mayor Gonnelli attempted to change the Inter-municipal Tax Sharing formula. This aspect of the enabling act has been the most controversial element of the enabling legislation. To this date, the formula has distributed almost $7.5 million between payers and receivers. The biggest payer is Secaucus, a contributor of almost $3 million, and the largest receiver is Kearny, getting close to $4 million each year.

Gonnelli threatened litigation based on a study commissioned by the payers regarding the formula, which indicated that the formula should have changed when the new master plan was adopted in 2004. Gonnelli was given assurances by the Christie administration that it would look at the tax sharing formula, and Assemblyman Vincent Prieto and state senator Paul Sarlo introduced several pieces of legislation to offset the impacts to the paying communities. Some of the bills called for surcharges on parking at MetLife Stadium and American Dream and on hotel rooms throughout the district. The Jets and Giants, which operate the stadium, fought hard to make sure no surcharges were imposed. They insisted that the lease they signed with the state would not allow for an additional surcharge and that if the state wanted the money, it should be deducted from the lease payment they already pay. Both legislators, chairman of their respective appropriation committees, were successful in funding the tax sharing impacts through the state budget process, but Gonnelli was looking for a permanent funding solution.

With all this happening, the Karrow/Gonnelli feud escalated with the mayor going every month to the commission meeting and pointing out Karrow's leadership shortfalls. In response, Karrow projected her anger at Gonnelli by screaming at him over the phone. In return, Karrow put out an edict to the commission staff that no one was to speak to Gonnelli or anyone associated with Secaucus even if he called them. Karrow was totally nonresponsive to developers dealing with projects, calls for a master plan revision by the chamber of commerce were pushed back and the transportation planning district regulations were allowed to expire. Compounding the morale problem with staff was the fact that the commission staff had not gotten a salary increase for more than six years. Karrow spent a great deal of time working from home because her commute from Flemington to Lyndhurst was long and tedious. The staff was left asking questions without getting answers. It was taking longer and longer to get things done. The commissioners of the agency dreaded commission days when Gonnelli listed his grievances or when they went into their communities and had to hear about the increasing amount of problems caused by the commission. Even though they may have wanted to replace Karrow, they were powerless. Though the commission has the authority to appoint the executive director, it is, in fact, the governor's choice.

The relations between constituent municipalities and the commission hit its lowest point since 1969, when the Meadowlands Act went into effect. It got so bad for Secaucus that Mayor Gonnelli alleged that Karrow was going out of her way to put up roadblocks on projects that Secaucus supported. Many mayors just refused to reach out to the commission. Unfortunately, the staff was always put in the middle of these controversies by following orders or when they were given no direction at all. One of Karrow's main tools of revenge was threatening ethics charges against someone who would challenge her.

With the New Jersey Sports and Exposition Authority winding down its statutory responsibility through the Christie administration and with the Hanson Commission providing guidance regarding the role of the authority, it was evident the end was near. With that in mind, both Prieto and Sarlo decided to introduce bills that would combine the NJSEA and NJMC into a new entity called the Meadowlands Regional Commission. The new agency would have an expanded board, including mayors. Under the Department of State, it would create a sports and entertainment district from the 750 acres of the complex; specifically outline mandates for environmental protection, flood control, environmental education and tourism; and allow municipalities to permit projects within their Meadowlands area if they adopted the NJMC master plan, zoning regulations and redevelopment plans. If the project required a variance, the commission staff would do the review and approval. Regarding tax sharing, the Prieto bill required a surcharge on hotel rooms to offset the costs of the payers in the formula. If the revenue was not sufficient, the state would cover the difference.

Both legislators introduced their bills in November and December. Once Prieto introduced his bill in the assembly, the quick movement on the bills was historic. To make sure the push for these bills would happen before the holiday recess in December, the bills were amended to make sure they were identical and that they incorporated amendments that were suggested by the governor's office. The key amendments were adopted so that rather than the sports authority being absorbed by the Meadowlands Commission, thus creating a new entity called the Meadowlands Regional Commission, it was reversed so the NJMC was taken over by the NJSEA. The NJSEA name and governing board remained the same. This was done at the request of American Dream, which expressed the concern that any changes would jeopardize its financing of the project.

Among the amendments was the inclusion of Liberty State Park under the jurisdiction of the new entity, which caused an uproar among environmental groups that have been trying to complete a master plan under the jurisdiction of the NJDEP for years. The language in questions says:

> *Evaluate, approve, and implement any plan or plans for the further preservation, development, enhancement, or improvement of Liberty State Park and the buildings, structures, properties, and appurtenances related thereto, or incidental to, necessary for, or complimentary to the park. The commission may avail itself of any plans under review by the Department of Environmental Protection from any source that may promote expanded and diverse recreational, cultural, and educational opportunities for visitors to Liberty State Park and provide greater access to park facilities. Any approved plans shall constitute a project of the commission, and shall be adopted as part of the master plan.*

There was a fear among members of the groups—especially Sam Pesin, head of the Friends of Liberty State Park, Debbie Mans and Greg Remaud of New York/New Jersey Baykeeper—that this move was the precursor to selling park assets to the private sector, which would drastically change the atmosphere of the park. It was acknowledged in published reports that the administration put the amendment into the bill but would not clarify the reasons why. Liberty State Park is about three or four miles from the jurisdiction of the Meadowlands district boundaries. Both sponsors promised language that would not endanger the park.

There was also a concern about the future of the Meadowlands Environmental Research Institute (MERI). Its purpose was to provide scientific data to the NJMC for policy development. MERI has also provided every constituent municipality with GIS systems and data. There was language in the bill that allowed MERI to operate under a not-for-profit organization. The purpose of the language was to allow MERI to move out from under the NJMC and to a college sponsor. Attempts to accomplish this logical progression were continually stymied by Marcia Karrow, who was more interested in making exorbitant cash from the transaction than making good public policy or letting the MERI scientists flourish with their groundbreaking research.

The other change was the language dealing with municipal authority to permit projects. This section was amended further to allow municipalities to grant bulk variance. A bulk variance allows the owner to use the land in a way that is not permitted by the zoning law. It is primarily used when a building application does not comply with the setback, height, lot or area requirements of a zoning ordinance. The language of the amendment allows the municipality to use the New Jersey Municipal Land Use Law (MLUL) language to make a decision. On the surface, it looks like a contradiction because the bill indicated that the towns had to adopted NJMC regulations to make their decisions. The one thing about the MLUL is the reasons to grant a bulk variance may be wider in scope compared to the Meadowlands Commission. So today, after forty-six years, the municipalities of the Meadowlands have some control over land use decisions if they want it. If a town does not want the control, it can continue to allow the authority to issue the permits. Some mayors have indicated they do not want the power so they can continue to blame the regional entity for approving controversial projects.

Members of the development community have expressed concerns about this change. The concerns were based on two areas: the time needed for getting approvals on a zoning certificate and the time it would take to go before a municipal planning board, which may or may not be equipped to hear the volume of applications, should the municipality opt in for this authority. This uncertainty has caused a level of consternation among the development community, which was accustomed to going before commission engineers and planning professionals—who would make the recommendations of approval or denial—as opposed to citizen planning boards in the towns. Only time will tell how this works out.

The tax sharing payers were satisfied that they would never have to pay into the fund again and, thus, realized instant property tax relief, and the receivers were satisfied that they would continue to receive the level of funding due them for not being able to develop in wetlands, open space or in areas impacted by old landfills. The hotel surcharge was in the bill, which caused the hotels and the Meadowlands chamber of commerce's convention and visitors' bureau concern about the competiveness of the Meadowlands hotels.

In the end, the Hackensack Meadowlands Agency Consolidation Act, the Hackensack Meadowlands Transportation Planning District Act of 2014 and the New Jersey Meadowlands Tax Relief Act went through both houses of the legislature in ten days. There were some who thought Governor Christie would conditionally veto the bill to eliminate some of the problematic language, but he signed the bill on February 5, 2015. With one stroke of the pen, the Meadowlands Commission was no more. What started out as looking for a solution for tax sharing ended up being the elimination of the Meadowlands Commission.

Governor Christie, Speaker Prieto and state senator Sarlo made statements that they are committed to a "clean up" bill that was, in fact, introduced the day the bill was signed. What is contained in that bill remains to be seen. Down the road, addition bills are sure to make language adjustments as the act is implemented.

There are those with the opinion that the Meadowlands Commission outlived its usefulness and that the grand vision of the 1970 master plan was no longer viable because it was created at a time that did not reflect the complexities of future impacts of federal and state environmental law. They say that land use goals of 1970 were unrealistic and did not take into consideration traffic and infrastructure conditions. While the 2004 master plan was a more realistic plan of the commission using its redevelopment powers to convert the older parts of the district into viable growth centers, the Great Recession that started in 2007–08 and Superstorm Sandy did not make it easy for the Meadowlands to accomplish what it sought in terms of land use successes.

There are those who contend that the constituent municipalities should not be trusted with land use authority because it was obvious they could not handle it before. The concern of igniting a ratable chase without regard to good planning has also been expressed, and the environmental community is concerned that the gains from the 2004 master plan will be lost. There is very specific language to make sure that does not happen, but human nature being what it is, we react to what might be before we actually see what is.

The concept of a new Meadowlands Regional Commission consolidating the NJMC and NJSEA into a superagency that would have handled master planning and redevelopment, flood control, infrastructure improvements, tourism and very specific environmental mandates for the first time, including for the 750 acres of the sports complex, would have been good for the region. In 1971, when the concept of the sports complex was discussed, the Meadowlands Commission attempted to be the lead agency responsible for all of it. Today, that is what we have.

What is going to happen to the former commission and its staff? The commission staff has never really been recognized outside the agency for the job they have done over the years. The core of the commission staff will be staying on to undertake the job they have been doing all along. Out of the fourteen constituent municipalities, only a handful will probably opt out and use their new powers under the statute. The balance will continue to have applicants go to the commission. Those that do opt out will need to be restructured so they can handle the workload of the new responsibilities.

Do they work out agreements with the new NJSEA to carry some of the workload, or do they even hire former NJMC staff members to assist in the review process? All of this still needs to be determined.

Some positions will probably be eliminated. Even though the act took effect immediately, there will be a transition period to work out the issues, and there will certainly be issues to work out with such a huge policy and regulatory shift.

But what is really the future of the Meadowlands region? One thing is for certain: the Meadowlands district cannot wait another five years for a new master plan. The new NJSEA needs to initiate that effort now to reflect what is about to happen in the region. The Meadowlands will continue to be the strong economic engine of northeast New Jersey. The infrastructure will make certain that logistics, distribution and warehousing will be even stronger in the future with the ports open to the new Panamax ships coming through the Panama Canal in the near future. Redevelopment areas will see new warehousing that will be more efficient

River Bend preserved wetlands in Secaucus near the Malanka landfill. *Courtesy of the New Jersey Meadowlands Commission.*

in space and automation. With the opening of American Dream, the Meadowlands will be a major tourism destination, which will lead to more hotels, other recreational opportunities and many new support service companies that will create more jobs. It was a sad day when the Izod Arena was closed recently in a deal with the Prudential Center in Newark. More than one thousand people lost their jobs with that announcement. It is hoped it will be reopened under the control of American Dream and be part of the new entertainment experience.

The discussion recently has surfaced about the licensing of two casinos, in the Meadowlands and in Jersey City. If a casino referendum is placed on the ballot, it will likely be successful. That could happen as early as November 2015. Should it pass, the sports complex will be the center of entertainment, and there will be positive spillover effect for all the other areas of the Meadowlands.

You can look at the glass half empty or half full. Visions for the Meadowlands have come and gone for more than three hundred years. Perhaps these new changes will provide the push needed to evolve the district into a higher and better place.

INDEX

A

B

C

D

ABOUT THE AUTHORS

Robert Ceberio is a longtime public servant specializing in land use, economic development and environmental protection. As executive director of the New Jersey Meadowlands Commission from 2002 to 2011, he brought that noted regional planning agency to the height of its influence and accomplishments. Now president of RCM Ceberio, LLC, he is assisting private entities and public agencies to achieve their goals and objectives in terms of new projects, institutional planning and policy decisions. Ceberio was an adjunct professor in the graduate schools of Fairleigh Dickinson University and Rutgers University teaching in the public administration, administrative sciences and the business administration programs. He is the author of articles and papers on environmental issues and regional planning models. His e-mail is rcmceberio@gmail.com.

Ron Kase is a sociologist who retired in 2013 after being associated for twenty-five years with Ramapo College of New Jersey, where he was associate vice-president for grants and sponsored programs and taught writing and project development for the graduate program in educational technology. He was a member of the social science faculty of the school of dentistry at Fairleigh Dickinson University and assistant provost of the Teaneck/Hackensack campus. He was a professor and chair of the human service and teacher education department at the New York City

College of Technology (CUNY). Kase has written three published novels, three regional history books and edited two social science supplementary texts. He is currently writing a novel set in the 1930s in Tampa, Florida. His e-mail is ronkase@rocketmail.com.